DANTE

AND

HIS EARLY BIOGRAPHERS

DANTE

AND

HIS EARLY BIOGRAPHERS

BY

EDWARD MOORE, D.D.

PRINCIPAL OF S. EDMUND HALL, OXFORD

AUTHOR OF "CONTRIBUTIONS TO THE TEXTUAL CRITICISM OF THE
DIVINA COMMEDIA," "TIME-REFERENCES IN THE DIVINA
COMMEDIA," ETC.

HASKELL HOUSE PUBLISHERS Ltd.
Publishers of Scarce Scholarly Books
NEW YORK, N. Y. 10012
1970

First Published 1889

HASKELL HOUSE PUBLISHERS LTD.
Publishers of Scarce Scholarly Books
280 LAFAYETTE STREET
NEW YORK. N. Y. 10012

Library of Congress Catalog Card Number: 70-122459

Standard Book Number 8383-1002-8
Printed in the United States of America

PREFACE

THIS book represents, in a somewhat expanded form, the substance of three Lectures which I delivered in 1889, as Barlow Lecturer on Dante in University College, London.

Though the plan of a great part of the work precludes much claim to originality, I believe the discussion of the authorship and mutual relation of the two forms of the Life of Dante attributed to Boccaccio will be entirely new to English readers. I cannot find, either from any published work, or from inquiry among fellow-students of Dante in England, that this curious problem has as yet received any attention in this country, though it has given rise to a great deal of discussion both in Italy and in Germany.

E. M.

S. EDMUND HALL, OXFORD,
Christmas Eve 1889.

CONTENTS

CHAPTER VII.

CHAPTER VIII.

CHAPTER I.

THE activity of Dante-scholars during the present century in producing biographies of the poet and in conducting researches and collecting materials in all quarters likely to throw light upon the events of his life has been scarcely less remarkable than that displayed in the multiplication of translations, editions, and commentaries. It is no depreciation of the merit of many of these excellent works to say that they can never displace, or deprive of their value and interest, the primitive and more nearly contemporary biographies, with the consideration of which we are now especially concerned. If one class of writings boasts the advantage of wider research into records and documents, the other may claim that of the contact of the living mind if not with the very person described, at least with those who knew him in the flesh. One class may display a more critical spirit, and a more judicial treatment of conflicting or doubtful evidence; the other has the freshness, simplicity, naturalness,

A

of a personal narrative unhampered by critical
misgivings and anxieties; one deals with its
subject as a man already illustrious, acting on the
stage of history, and, as it were, before the eyes of
men; the other sees him more as a man living
and acting among his fellow-men, who are as yet
unconscious or only half-conscious that "there is
a prophet among them." As a consequence, the
one deals mainly with the more important and
public incidents of his career, the other lingers
over his private life and his personal and domestic
intercourse. The latter tends, therefore, to be
anecdotal (some might perhaps say gossiping),
preserving details which, though trivial in themselves, yet make the picture a more real and living
one. These "little nameless unremembered acts"
clothe for us, as it were with flesh and skin, the
skeleton which has been preserved in the museum
of history. Thus it is that the two classes of
lives, the ancient and the modern, exhibit different
types, each having its own peculiar value and
interest. The existence of the one does not
supersede the other in either direction. They
are supplementary, rather than alternative. One
gives us a history, the other a portraiture; the
one a Biography, the other a Life.

The works which may claim to fall under the
description of early biographies are, I think, five
in number, their authors being, (1) Boccaccio;
(2) Lionardo Aretino; (3) Filippo Villani; (4)
Manetti; (5) Filelfo. The dates of the actual

composition of these works being uncertain, those of their authors' lives are here given. Boccaccio, 1313-1375; Villani, date of birth uncertain (but before 1348), died about 1404; Lionardo, 1369-1444; Manetti, 1396-1459; Filelfo, 1426-1480. Our plan will be first to give some account of each of these works in order, noticing their special characteristics or purpose, and the qualifications of the authors for their task in respect of personal knowledge, access to other sources of information, critical faculty, and so forth. After this it is proposed to take a general view of the body of information thus transmitted to us as to personal characteristics and details respecting Dante, supplementing or illustrating such information by passages occurring in his own writings.

CHAPTER II.

IT is needless to point out the peculiar advantages possessed by Boccaccio as a biographer of the poet. He was born during Dante's lifetime,

"ancorchè fosse tardi,"

too late indeed for personal knowledge of him, though not too late to have intercourse and acquaintance with those who knew him familiarly, at a time consequently when in living memories there existed a store of anecdotes and personal reminiscences of the man as he lived and moved among his fellows, of the aspect he wore to them, of the impression he made upon them. Boccaccio had also another qualification, that of

"lungo studio e grande amore,"

in respect of the poet and his works. When the Florentines in 1373 determined to establish a public Lectureship[1] on Dante, Boccaccio was appointed to the office, and delivered his first Lecture on October 12 in that year, in the Church of San Stefano, near the Ponte Vecchio. His

[1] The example thus set by Florence was followed later by Pisa, Piacenza, Ferrara, Bologna, Milan, Venice, and, I believe, Ravenna. (See Supplementary Notes.)

Lectures took the form of a minute and elaborate Commentary, which is preserved to us as a fragment only, since his work was unhappily interrupted by death in December 1375, when his Commentary had reached the 17th line of the 17th Canto of the *Inferno.* The language of this Commentary is (as one might say) saturated with Dantesque phraseology; the frequency of apparently unconscious quotations of phrases and expressions indicates a very thorough acquaintance with all parts of the *Divina Commedia.*[1] We know him to have had personal communication with one at least of the children of Dante, his daughter Beatrice, a nun in the convent of San Stefano dell' Uliva at Ravenna, for he was commissioned by a decree of the citizens of Florence (or, to speak more precisely, the company of Or San Michele), in the year 1350, to convey to her a subsidy of ten florins of gold.[2] Other personal sources of information will be mentioned later.

But we are met at the outset by a very curious difficulty. What was the Life of Dante which Boccaccio really wrote? Two works, having large portions in common and large portions peculiar to each, have come down to us, the exact relation of which to one another, and of either or both to their reputed author Boccaccio, long has been, and still is, a matter of dispute. This subject has been very often discussed, among others by Dr.

---

[1] The same remark applies also to the *poetical* works of Boccaccio.   [2] Pelli, *Memorie*, p. 45.

Witte (in No. vii. of the second series of his *Dante Forschungen*), also by Schaeffer-Boichorst in *Aus Dante's Verbannung*, pp. 191-226, and the whole controversy has been carefully gone over again in a lengthy and elaborate work by Macrì-Leone, published as lately as 1888.

It is to be observed that there are at least two other minor forms or recensions of the Life by Boccaccio occurring in some MSS. It will be enough, however, for us to consider the case of the two principal forms, each of which claims to be *the* Vita di Boccaccio, and each of which has found distinguished advocates. One being on the whole longer than the other, though some separate episodes are treated at greater length in the shorter form (so that one is not a mere epitome of the other), it has been usual to speak of the longer as the *Vita*, and the shorter as the *Compendio*. It will be convenient for purposes of reference to adopt this nomenclature, without thereby prejudging the question of their relative claims. Some have maintained that the *Vita* is the original work, and that the *Compendio* is a modification of it, executed either by the author himself or by some one else (for which special reasons, based on internal evidence, are in both cases suggested). Others (though very few) have supposed the so-called *Compendio* to be the original, and the *Vita* to be an expansion of it, carried out in one or other of the two ways suggested in the former case.

Critics then fall under four classes :—

I. Those who hold the *Vita* to be genuine and the *Compendio* spurious, *i.e.* an unauthorised *rifacimento*. This is the opinion most commonly held, and the following are its principal adherents :—Biscioni (who first called attention to the question), Pelli, Tiraboschi, Gamba, Baldelli, Ugo Foscolo, Paur, Witte (though hesitating as to condemning the *Compendio*), Scartazzini,[1] Koerting, and the last writer on the subject, Macrì-Leone, to whom I am mainly indebted for the list just given.[2]

II. Those who hold the *Compendio* to be genuine and the *Vita* spurious (in the sense given above). This singular view seems to have been maintained (as far as I can ascertain) only by Dionisi and Mussi. The latter is the editor of the magnificent edition of 1809 (the pages of which measure about 23 inches by 15, and of which only 72 copies were printed). In this the so-called *Compendio* is included, and it was then first published.

III. Those who believe both to be genuine, the *Vita* the original, and the *Compendio* a revision by the author. This is maintained with much vigour by Schaeffer-Boichorst.

[1] See *Vita di Dante, Manuali Hoepli*, p. 7.

[2] It has even been absurdly suggested that the *Compendio* was the work of Giovanni da Serravalle, the author of the well-known Commentary, though the two works contradict one another on an important question of fact. See Macrì-Leone, *Introduction*, p. xiii, and *inf.* p. 10.

IV. Those who adopt the converse view to this, regarding the *Compendio* as a sort of first draft or outline sketch, and the *Vita* a later expansion, or more complete work by the same author. This is the opinion of the editors of the Paduan edition of 1822.

Without attempting fully to argue out this difficult question, I shall hope later on to indicate what are the principal landmarks of the controversy, after giving a rapid sketch of the contents of the Life or Lives now before us, a course which I propose to adopt. in the case of the other four early biographies also. I shall follow the outlines of the *Vita Intera*, noting, as we go on, the principal instances of divergence, either in the way of omission or expansion, occurring in the *Compendio*. We shall then be better able to appreciate the nature of the problem, and the chief points that have to be taken account of in its solution. I will only premise (as it will tend to concentrate the attention on differences that bear on the question), that the conclusion to which we shall be led is that the *Vita* at any rate is certainly genuine, and that the only question practically is as to the relation which the *Compendio* bears to it, *i.e.* whether it is an authorised or an unauthorised recension. I will also further add, that I am decidedly of the latter opinion.

In the first chapter, we meet at once with a conspicuous instance of the most characteristic point of difference between the two Lives, and that in which alone any very decided motive can be traced. I mean the omission or softening down of some very vigorous denunciations of Florence, which occur several times in the *Vita.* One of the bitterest of these well-deserved invectives is found in this first chapter. In the *Compendio* it is very much abbreviated, and its severest expressions excised.

In the second chapter, we have an account of the origin of Dante's family, from the union of Cacciaguida (of the family of the Elisei, who came of the ancient stock of the Frangipani from Rome) with a daughter of the Aldighieri[1] (for so Boccaccio says that the name was originally spelt) from Ferrara.[2] It is curious to note the repetition of the error, common at that time, that Florence was destroyed by Attila, "the most cruel king of the Vandals," instead of Totila. This is found too in Dante, *Inf.* xiii. 149, and the early Commentators are also in confusion on the subject.[3] We find moreover the blunder (which is repeated by Benvenuto da Imola, and others), that Dante was born in 1265 *sedente Urbano papa IV.* This should be *Clemente IV.,* since

---

[1] Compare F. Villani's opinion on this, *inf.* pp. 59, 60.

[2] See Supplementary Notes.

[3] In Boccaccio's Commentary on *Inf.* xii. 134, Attila is described as king of the Goths, and the question as between Attila and Totila is also noticed in a confused way. See also *inf.* p. 40, and Supplementary Notes.

Urban IV. died Oct. 2, 1264.[1] The future poet's education and early devotion to study are then noticed. For this purpose he spent some time at Bologna, and also later, and when drawing near to old age (*vicino alla sua vecchiezza*),[2] he went as far as Paris, where he disputed with such skill as to astonish his hearers.[3]

There is an interesting notice (omitted, by the way, in the *Compendio*) of Dante's special devotion to Virgil, Horace, Ovid, and Statius, his minute acquaintance with whom is said to be displayed by frequent imitations in his own

[1] A marvellous vision seen by Dante's mother, shortly before his birth, is described here in the *Vita*, while in the *Compendio* a description is merely promised later. This promise is fulfilled in chapter xvii., where the account is repeated in the *Vita* also. This is certainly in favour at any rate of the *priority* of the *Vita*. The epitomiser (whether Boccaccio or another) having noticed the useless repetition of this narrative, naturally corrected the flaw by its omission in this place, and by substituting the promise of a reference to it later. The converse process, implying its needless introduction here, would surely be quite unintelligible.

[2] These words *vicino alla sua vecchiezza* should be specially noticed, since the visit to Paris, according to Serravalle (the sole authority for Dante's supposed visit to Oxford), took place in his youth, when he would have obtained at Paris a degree, for which he had fully qualified himself *sed deerat sibi pecunia*, and he consequently returned to Florence to obtain the necessary funds, but he there became entangled in public life, and so never returned to claim his degree.

[3] This visit to Paris is again described in its proper place in chapter v., and also in nearly similar language in the *Lezione Prima* of Boccaccio's Commentary.

works. This is entirely true, though less re-
markably so in the case of Horace than of the
others.[1]

In Chapter III. we have the account of Dante's
devotion to Beatrice, and of his own marriage,
shortly after her death, with Gemma Donati.
Here, be it observed, occurs Boccaccio's statement
of the family name of Beatrice, to which *and
to which alone* we owe the knowledge that she
was the daughter of Folco Portinari.[2] Dante
himself never gives us any clue to her family
name, nor, I think, does he even definitely
state that she lived in Florence; he merely
speaks of the " city in which God had placed
my lady " (see *Vita Nuova, c.* vi., and compare
c. xli. *init.*).

The curiously ambiguous language in which
she is first mentioned in the beginning of the
Vita Nuova will be in the memory of all—*la
gloriosa donna di mia mente, la quale fu chia-
mata da molti Beatrice, i quali non sapeano che si
chiamare.* Well does Boccaccio with strongest
emphasis insist that this affection was most

---

[1] See Supplementary Notes.

[2] Boccaccio gives us further details about her in his Commentary on *Inf.* ii. 57, and especially as to her marriage
with Simone de' Bardi. He says that it is worth while to
enter into these particulars, because Dante *non sempre
di lei allegoricamente favelli.* He adds also his authority
for what he states, viz. that it was *secondo la relazione
di fededegna persona, la quale la conobbe, e fu per consanguinità strettissima a lei.* (See further Supplementary Notes.)

honourable, and that never by look, or word, or sign, either on the part of the lover, or on that of the object of his love, was there the slightest admixture of sensuous passion. But later on in the chapter, after a description more or less common to both works, though the actual language is different, of Dante's grief at the loss of Beatrice, when he was twenty-four years of age, there occurs one of the most important divergences between the two Lives, and I venture to think one of the passages most fatal to the credit of the *Compendio*. Both works describe the gradual recovery of Dante from the first crushing effects of grief, and how his friends took counsel together to provide him with a wife, in order that his strong affections might be diverted into another channel. But the *Compendio* inserts an offensive passage, quite out of place moreover in the sequence of the history, how that Dante recovered so completely from his sorrow, that *in his later years* he sighed after many other objects of affection, and especially *after his exile*, in Lucca, for a young girl, whom he names [1] *Pargoletta*. Moreover Boccaccio himself was aware that *pargoletta* was not a proper name, for later on, in *this same chapter* in the *Vita*, though not in the *Compendio*, the phrase occurs *in sua pargoletta età*. The

---

[1] This expression "whom he names" betrays with charming *naïveté* the source of the writer's statement to be a perverted recollection and combination of the two passages, *Purg.* xxiv. 34-6, and xxxi. 59.

writer proceeds further: " besides that, near the end of his life (*vicino allo stremo di sua vita*) in the mountains of the Casentino, he became attached to an Alpine damsel, who, if I am not mistaken, though she had a good-looking face, had a *goître*! and he composed for one or other of these girls a great number of excellent verses." But enough of this. If Boccaccio had heard of this stuff, and had the bad taste to believe and to record it, he is not likely to have come by the knowledge *only late in his life*, and when further removed in time from the supposed occurrences. (I am here taking for granted, what is in fact the only tenable view, that the *Compendio*, if genuine at all, which I do not believe, is certainly the *later* work.) This is, in fact, just such expansive gossip as is apt to grow up round the simple statements of early and genuine records. It is thus that fancy often fills in the details of pictures which truth has tantalisingly left in mere outline. Compare, for instance, the loquacity of the spurious Gospels of the Infancy with the reticence of the genuine Gospels; or St. John's simple narrative of the Resurrection of Lazarus with the voluble details of later tradition.

This chapter (which appears to have been more extensively remodelled throughout by the reviser than any other) is distinguished by another feature which is specially marked in the *Compendio*, and which reappears afterwards more than once, viz. extremely violent, and at the

same time humorous, denunciations of married
life, and the assertion of the utter unsuitability
of that estate for philosophers, or any others with
a serious work or purpose in life. Some of these
passages are sufficiently amusing to be worth
quoting, and they are curiously modern in tone.

The first rumblings of the coming storm are
heard at the beginning of the chapter, where
both Lives mention, among other interruptions to
Dante's studies, that he had a wife; but the
Compendio also feelingly adds, " and what prime
enemies wives are of philosophic studies, they
know who have experienced it "! The full force
of the storm bursts forth a little later, *à propos* of
the injudicious advice given to Dante by his
friends, that he should cure his grief at the loss
of Beatrice by taking to himself a wife. People
do not consider (as the writer euphemistically
puts it) " what a dangerous step it is to quench
a temporary fire by a lasting one." " His love
for Beatrice was indeed a heavy burden for him
to bear, but it was not without the compensa-
tion of many sweet thoughts, . . . whereas the
companionship of a wife, as they affirm who have
experienced it, brings nothing but constant
anxiety and unremitting strife." Then follows a
most humorous description of the hindrances to
Dante's studies, arising from his wife's complaints of his unsociable habits, from her troublesome interruption of his sublimest speculations
by inviting his attention to the payment of the

nurses' wages, and seeing to the children's clothes.

In justice to Boccaccio, it should be observed that the undoubtedly genuine *Vita* does not at all fall short in the decision or severity of its sentiments on this interesting subject. His opinion is expressed with equal vigour, though he does not enter with quite such raciness into the details of domestic management; but that, like the penitent Falstaff on his deathbed, he does "in some sort, indeed, handle women," will appear from the following extracts.

After noting similarly the objection that wives have to the studious habits of their husbands, and pointing out how sadly the married man is hampered in the freedom of his outside intercourse, how he has to render an account to his wife not only of his more serious actions, but even of every little sigh on which he may have ventured, he pitifully exclaims, "O the incalculable weariness of having such a suspicious creature to live with, to converse with, and at last to grow old with, and even to die with! . . . How angry they get, if they do not receive constant attention! There is no brute more cruel than, no, nor so cruel as, an angry woman. No one can feel safe who commits himself to the power of any woman who thinks she has good reason to be annoyed, and they all think that." After a little more in this strain, he pulls himself up with the reflection (which, it must be admitted, occurs to him rather

late) that it is of no use proving at length what
every one knows, and that he judges it better to
hold his tongue than to run the risk of offending,
by speaking, the fair ladies (*le vaghe donne*). He
will only add that he considers it utterly prepos-
terous that of all things in the world a wife is
the only one that a man is willing to take without a previous trial.[1] He finally defends himself (and this passage occurs in both' the works)
with well-feigned gravity from being thought an
enemy to marriage generally. "On the contrary,"
he says, "I commend it, but not for every òne.
Philosophers should leave it to gentlemen and to
rich fools, and also to the working classes; considering themselves to be much better and more
agreeably married to philosophy."[2]

The *Vita* also adds a more important and
serious reservation which ' is omitted in the

[1] This reflection is repeated and amplified in *Comento*
(*Lez.* 58), where examples are added of things we should not
think of taking without trial, such as horses, asses, cattle,
dogs, the commonest servants, clothes, chairs, etc. etc.
This passage in particular, as well as a good deal besides in
this chapter, is little else than a translation of a fragment
of the lost work of Theophrastus, περὶ γάμου, which is
preserved in a translation by S. Jerome, *adv. Jovinianum*,
Lib. i. vol. ii. p. 314; ed. Verona, 1734-42. In the *Comento*
(*l.c.*) Boccaccio acknowledges his obligation to that work.

[2] In the *Comento, Lez.* xi. (i. p. 304) Boccaccio says that
"Eve was taken out of Adam's side to show that God intended woman to be neither the mistress nor the slave of man,
but his companion ; and that He gave her to Adam as a source
of solace and comfort, not for perpetual anxiety and for war
without peace and without truce, as I hear is the case with

Compendio, viz. that as far as Dante ·is con
cerned, this is nothing but an imaginary picture.
"I certainly," he adds, "do not say that all this
happened in Dante's case, because I do not know
it (*chè nol so*); but it seems that something like
this must have occurred to account for the fact
that Dante, when once parted from his wife,
who, it will ˙be remembered, had been supplied
to him as a consolation in trouble, never went
near her again, or allowed her to come near him."

·The author of the *Compendio* bluntly adduces
this circumstance as proof that the foregoing
description of married life was applicable to
Dante's case, omitting the warning that the
writer had no definite knowledge on the subject.
"Whatever," he says, "other wives may be, . . .
such was she who was given to Dante, that when
he once left her," etc.

No doubt this last fact is a difficult one to get
over,[1] and so also is the complete absence of any

wives of the present day." There is also a long and singular
outbreak very like this chapter both in its general feeling and
also in particular phrases and expressions in the Commentary
(*Lez.* 58), *à propos* of *Inf.* xvi. 45, when Jacopo Rusticucci,
in the spirit of our first parent Adam, attributes his condemnation to the woman that "was given to be with him".
La fiera moglie più che altro mi nuoce. Boccaccio seems
to think this likely and natural enough.

[1] It may be noted that in the *Vita*, Chapter v., the chari-
table suggestion is made that Dante's children were too young
to accompany him on his flight (*male per picciola età alla fuga
disposta*), and also that he could leave his wife without
anxiety for her safety by reason of her connection with some

allusion by Dante to his wife, children, or
domestic life in the *Commedia* or any other
of his writings, unless we except the tender
reference in *Par.* xvii. 55 to the separation from
every object most dearly loved as the first wound
that exile inflicts.[1]   Still, from all we know of his
character and disposition, Dante was probably
what Aristotle would call χαλεπὸς πρὸς τὸ συμ-
βιοῦν, "not an easy man to get on with"; so that
if there really was unhappiness in his married
life, it by no means follows that the fault was
altogether on his wife's side, or that Boccaccio's
inference and conjecture (for it is admittedly no
more) is true.   It is likely enough however that she
was not exactly "a help meet for him".   She probably had little sympathy with his enthusiasms,
and little capacity for sharing in his intellectual or
literary pursuits.   Indeed, Dante's opinion of the
intellectual capacity of the "nobler sex", whether
derived from his experience of Gemma, or otherwise, was not much higher than that of Boccaccio.
This will appear from some passages which I
shall have to quote later on.   Still there is no
doubt that poor Gemma Donati's memory has
suffered severely, and as far as we know un-
deservedly, from the inaccurate notion that all
this tirade in Boccaccio is a description of *her*
of the leaders of the other faction (she being of course a
Donati).   This is significantly omitted in the *Compendio.*

[1] The omission of any mention of *wives* in *Par.* xiv. 64, 65,
has sometimes been remarked upon.   It was perhaps forgotten that the spirits here are those of the great *Theologians* !

conduct in particular. This is most distinctly not the case, as Boccaccio himself candidly warns us. It has been common, for instance, to compare Dante with Socrates and his domestic scourge, Xanthippe. We cannot now go further into this question, but I would refer my readers to a very interesting paper, in which the subject is discussed with his usual clearness and thoroughness, by Dr. Witte, *Dante-Forschungen,* II. No. vi. I will only add that, among the Lives which we shall consider later, Lionardo protests against all this part of Boccaccio's Life as fantastic gossip, while Manetti illustrates the habit of later writers, which I have already stigmatised, by exaggerating and amplifying the imaginary picture of Boccaccio to the further discredit of Gemma.

But we have lingered too long over these fascinating passages of Chapter III., and we must proceed with our sketch.

In Chapter IV. we are told that Dante, to divert himself from the cares of domestic life, plunged with absorbing fervour into public affairs, and this is described at greater length in the *Compendio.* This is followed by a description of factions at Florence, and their bitter conflicts, ending in the defeat and exile of Dante and his party. Then occurs in the *Vita* a long and bitter invective against Florence, characteristically omitted in the *Compendio.*

Chapter V. describes the wanderings of Dante's

exile. His first refuge was at Veroña. The *Vita*
definitely states that it was with Alberto della
Scala, while the *Compendio* substitutes the cautious
phrase, *il signore della terra.* It is still disputed *which* della Scala was the *gran Lombardo* of
Par. xvii. 71, but it seems that it could not in
any case have been Alberto, since he died in
1301 (Sept. 10).[1] Indeed this appears to be clearly
one of the instances in which Boccaccio's statements are mere hasty inferences from passages
in Dante's own writings: in this case from
Par. xvii. 70, the very words *nel primo fuggire*
being an almost direct reproduction of *Lo primo
tuo rifugio.* Moreover, though this may have
been Dante's *primo rifugio,* it would not be true
to say that it was *nel primo fuggire.* Some
time elapsed first; see for instance the fuller
details given by Lionardo (*inf.* p. 74). Thence
in succession he sojourned in Tuscany, the
Casentino (with Count Salvatico), the Lunigiana
(with Moruello Malaspina), the neighbourhood
of Urbino (with Uguccione della Faggiuola), next
at Bologna, Padua, and Verona again, and then
after some years he went to Paris, and abandoned
himself wholly to the study of philosophy and
theology. All these names and details are
common to both works. He was recalled to
Italy and to thoughts of politics by the hopes
inspired by the election as Emperor of Henry of

[1] It is generally agreed that he is referred to in *Par.* xviii.
121, as having already (*i.e.* in 1300) " one foot in the grave ".

Luxemburg with the support (as we may add) at
first of the Pope Clement v. The poet's hopes
were once more, and now irretrievably, crushed
by the death of Henry vii. on Aug. 24, 1313,
and he took refuge in Romagna, and finally in
Ravenna, whither he was specially invited by
Guido Novello da Polenta, under whose protection he remained until his death.

The chapter concludes in both cases with a
summary of the difficulties with which the poet
had to contend, and a very just expression of
wonder and admiration at all that he accom-
plished in spite of them. The author of the
Compendio, as in Chapter iii., enters into more
detail, and also cannot help bringing into pro-
minence once more, among his disadvantages,
gli stimoli della moglie (words deliberately in-
serted in a sentence otherwise identical in both
works), whereas in the *Vita* we do not get nearer
to this than the general and harmless expression
la sollecitudine casalinga. In the *Compendio*
we have also an amusing contrast between Dante
working, thinking, and writing in the midst of
all these cares, sufferings, and obstacles, and the
ordinary run of students, who cannot either
think, or read, or write, unless they have a
comfortable chair, and a rest for their elbows,
and are not disturbed by the slightest sound.
Then the *Vita* proceeds to draw the very hazard-
ous and improbable inference that if, instead of
these drawbacks, Dante had had correspondingly

great advantages, or at least no difficulties to contend with, we could scarcely place any limit to
the greatness he would have achieved, *io direi,
che egli fosse in terra divenuto uno Iddio.*   But
assuredly his was a character that *could* be
formed only in the school of adversity.   Much
truer is the poet's own estimate of these things
in *Inf.* xxiv. 47, etc.—

> " sedendo in piuma,
> In fama non si vien, nè sotto coltre,
> Senza la qual, chi sua vita consuma,
> Cotal vestigio in terra di sè lascia,
> Qual fummo in aer, ed in acqua la schiuma."

Or again—if we may borrow the language of the
Latin poet, while we are contending against the
sentiment with which it is connected—in the case
imagined by the biographer—

> " caderent omnes a crinibus hydri,
> Surda nihil gemeret grave buccina ". [1]

Villani, in a somewhat similar passage, more
truly observes—*in ipso fortunae saevientis sinu
semper meliora dictabat.*

In Chapter vi. we are briefly but pathetically
told, " On the 14th of September 1321, the day on
which we celebrate the exaltation of the Sacred
Cross . . . he rendered up to God his weary
spirit, which I doubt not was received into the
arms of his most noble Beatrice, with whom, in
the sight of Him who is the Highest Good, having

---

[1] Juv. vii. 70-1.

escaped the miseries of this present life, he now lives most joyously in that of whose felicity we believe there shall be no end." Then follow details as to his burial, and the inscription on his tomb, which I have discussed at length elsewhere,[1] and which I now therefore pass over.

It is noticeable that we have no mention of the cause of his death, as to which we shall find more details in the Life by Villani.

Then follows in Chapter VII. another fierce denunciation of the ingratitude, madness, and cruelty of Florence towards the best and most distinguished of her citizens. This long chapter, extending over several pages, is reduced (as we should now be prepared to expect) in the *Compendio* to a few lines, though these are not wanting, as far as they go, in severity of expression.

The succeeding Chapter (VIII.) on the *Fattezze, Usanze e Costumi di Dante* is considerably abbreviated in various ways in the *Compendio*, but especially by omitting the story illustrating his power of mental abstraction; viz. how that at Siena, when a book of some celebrity which he had not before seen was brought to him in an apothecary's shop, he sat down at once to read it, and was so completely absorbed in it that he never so much as noticed the gay and tumultuous procession of a great *festa* which

---

[1] See an Article on "The Tomb of Dante" in the *English Historical Review* for January 1889.

passed by meanwhile.[1]　There is also similarly
an anecdote of a disputation at Paris (to which
the *Compendio* contains a mere allusion), in which·
Dante displayed a power of memory which appeared almost miraculous to the bystanders.
I pass over here the details of this chapter, as
they will be given later among the personal
characteristics and traits of the poet preserved
to us in the early biographies generally.

In the very long digression on poetry and
on the difference between poetry and theology,
which follows in Chapters IX. and X., there are
very considerable alterations in the *Compendio*,
both in the way of omission, expansion, and
general remodelling, the result being a slight
increase of its length, but with the loss, especially
in the latter part, of several graceful and epigram-
matic remarks.[2]　*E.g.*: the advantage of poetical
or allegorical teaching in matters both sacred
and profane is that it costs some mental effort

[1] Something curiously like this is related of Warburton.
" His absorption in books is illustrated by a story told of his
going to dine at Lord Tyrconnel's at Bilton Hall when a
fire was raging at a house which Warburton had to pass on
the road. . . . When he arrived at Bilton he had nothing
to tell : though he had ridden close by the house, he had
not noticed the fire."—Mark Pattison's *Essays*, ii. p. 122.

[2] Many of these, it must be admitted, are freely borrowed
from a letter of Petrarch.　A very similar passage occurs in
the Commentary, *Lez.* iii., *à propos* of the words *Poeta fui*
(*Inf.* i. 73).　In that case, however, the obligation is acknow-
ledged : *secondo che il mio padre e maestro messer Francesco
Petrarca scrive a Gherardo suo fratello.*

to make it one's own, and it is a fact of common experience that we value everything that has cost us some trouble more than that which comes to us without any effort. Thus it is that plain and direct statements of truth pass out of the mind as quickly and easily as they passed into it. Again, considering how allegory and parable are employed by our Lord Himself, and by the Holy Spirit speaking to us in Scripture, and on the other hand how much religious truth is conveyed by the teaching of heathen poets,[1] we may boldly say that " not only is poetry theology, but also that theology is poetry ". . . . . " I will even say," he adds, " that theology is nothing else than a poetry of God "—*la teologia niun' altra cosa è che una poesia di Dio.* We have in the *Compendio* a very poor and prosy substitute for these terse and pointed, even if not altogether original, conclusions.[2]

---

[1] Boccaccio declaims at much length in his Commentary (*Lez.* iii.) against the *dictum* of St. Jerome that the writings of the poets are *daemonum cibus. Inter alia,* he uses the curious argument that the words used by our Lord in Acts ix. 5, " It is hard for thee to kick against the pricks," are found in Terence. " Far be it from me," says Boccaccio, " to suggest that our Lord quoted Terence; but we may infer that he used language already found in Terence to show that the works of heathen poets are not to be thus condemned."

[2] The digression concludes in Chapter XI. with an account, common to both narratives, of the practice in Greece and Rome of crowning poets with laurel, an honour which Dante eagerly desired. The reference here is to the correspondence in the form of Eclogues between Dante and his friend

In Chapter XII., on the "qualities and defects of Dante", the *Compendio* considerably softens the language used about Dante's indignant repudiation of the unworthy conditions under which a return to Florence was proposed to him, which are well known from one of his extant epistles (No. x. *Ed.* Fraticelli). Immediately after this the well-known story is narrated in both works of the embassy to Boniface, when Dante expressed hesitation about accompanying it, with the proud saying, " If I go, who remains ? and if I remain, who goes ? " It is perhaps noticeable that the *Vita* explicitly states that this was when Boniface interfered with the affairs of our city by sending a brother, or some relation (this vagueness is curious) of Philip, then king of France, whose name was Charles. This refers of course to the threatened arrival in Florence of Charles of Valois, which took place in November 1301, and was the immediate cause of Dante's exile. The *Compendio* here substitutes the general phrase, *per alcuna gran bisogna, ambasciata a Bonifazio.* The *Vita* then briefly describes the Guelf and Ghibelline [1] factions by which Florence, as well as nearly all Tuscany and Lombardy, was dis-

Giovanni del Virgilio, in which Giovanni urges that Dante should consent to receive this honour at Bologna, while Dante utterly refuses to accept it anywhere but at Florence, a proud resolve which also finds expression in the well-known lines at the beginning of *Par.* xxv.

[1] The writer professes himself unable to explain the origin of these names.

tracted. This is omitted altogether in the *Compendio*. Both, however, mention the change of Dante from Guelphism to fierce Ghibellinism—greatly overstating the case, I should say—so much so that (as both record, with some apology for doing so, because his scornful eye is perhaps at the moment turned upon the writer from the heights of heaven) his temper on this subject was so ungovernable that he would throw stones at any one, even if it were a poor woman or child, who dared to irritate him by saying a word in depreciation of the Ghibellines. Then follows in both the celebrated and often quoted statement, *in questo mirifico Poeta trovò ampissimo luogo la lussuria, e non solamente ne' giovani anni ma ancora ne' maturi.*[1]

We then have in the *Vita* a curious passage entirely omitted in the *Compendio*. The writer of the former (*i.e.*, as we maintain, Boccaccio himself) proceeds: "This vice, though natural, and common, and almost necessary, in truth cannot be commended, and cannot even worthily be excused. But who among mortals is a just judge to condemn it ?" There surely speaks poor Boccaccio *ex animo*, showing the traces both of his unregenerate and his reformed life. He is said (it should be remembered) to have been converted from his evil ways and entirely reformed in 1361 through the influence of one

[1] We shall consider the weight of this charge of immorality of life later on. See p. 151.

Gioachino Ciani (see Witte, *Dante-Forschungen*, ii. p. 116). This is followed by some singular reflections on the weakness of man before the overpowering and irresistible influence of women, a point which is illustrated by instances from sacred and profane literature, such as Jupiter, Hercules, Paris, David, Solomon, and Herod.[1]

In the next Chapter (XIII.), on the various works of Dante, the *Compendio* omits two statements about the *Vita Nuova* found in the other work : (1) that Dante composed it in about his twenty-sixth year, and (2) that in his maturer years he was much ashamed of it. Boccaccio, notwithstanding, thinks it a very creditable work considering his age when it was written, and that it is *assai bello e piacevole, e massimamente ai volgari.* The second of the above statements, that Dante was ashamed of the *Vita Nuova*, seems entirely unfounded. For unless Boccaccio had some evidence, with which we are not acquainted, of a change of sentiment very late in Dante's life, it is quite inconsistent with his language in the *Convito*, I. i. "The present work called the *Convito* is a more manly treatise than the *Vita Nuova.* I do not intend, however, in any way to depreciate the latter (*a quella in alcuna parte*

---

[1] The curious balancing of instances from sacred and profane history should be noticed. It will be remembered that this is common in Dante himself, especially in the *Purgatorio.* See my *Time-References*, p. 133, and also Table VII. Also add to the instances there given—*Purg.* xxx. 19 and 21 *Par.* v. 66-72.

derogare), but rather to help out (*giovare*) that work by this." Moreover, twice besides in the *Convito* he refers back to statements or descriptions to be found in the *Vita Nuova* (II. ii. *init.*, and II. xiii. *med.*). It seems most likely, as Macrì-Leone suggests (p. cxiv), that this is a hasty inference from an imperfect recollection of the passage in the *Convito*; the expression *nel Convito si tratta piu virilmente che nella Vita Nuova* being remembered, but not the words which follow.

Then follows a long account of the undertaking of the *Commedia* (compressed into four or five lines in the *Compendio*), stating *inter alia* that it was commenced by Dante in his thirty-fifth year; but that its composition occupied the rest of his life; though he was employed at the same time with other literary labours. It is evident that Boccaccio here confuses the date poetically assumed for the vision with that of the actual composition of the work.[1] In Chapter XIV. in both works the stories are given of the interruption of the poem after *Inferno*, canto VII., owing to the author's exile and the temporary loss of that portion of the poem; and also that of the disappearance of the last thirteen cantos of the *Paradiso*, and their mysterious recovery eight months after the poet's death. These accidents

---

[1] This is a common error. It is found again in Manetti, and even more definitely in Serravalle's unpublished Commentary, since he says that Dante began his great work in 1300, *de mense Marcii, in die Veneris sancta, sc. in Parasceue.*

are there explained to be due to Dante's habit
—whenever he had finished seven or eight cantos,
more or less—of sending them to Can Grande
della Scala before any one else saw them, and after
that of allowing any one who wished to see them
(*ne facea copia a chi la ne voleva*).   This is
curious and interesting, and I have sometimes
thought it might throw light on the singular
relationships and divergences between MSS. not
only in the several *Cantiche*, but in groups or blocks
of cantos in the same *Cantica*.   I have not, however, succeeded in working out this idea in detail.

It is interesting to compare the differences of
detail in the three narratives of the recovery of
the first seven cantos in the *Vita*, the *Compendio*,
and the Commentary of Boccaccio on *Inferno* viii. I.
In the first named we are told, vaguely, that the
discovery was made by *alcuno per alcuna sua
scrittura forse a lui opportuna cercando fra cose di
Dante*.   Next, this person took the document
when found to Dino di messer Lambertuccio, a
famous poet in Florence at that time.   Thirdly,
he sent them, not to Dante himself, but to
Moruello Malaspina, with whom Dante was then
sojourning.   Finally, Moruello handed them to
Dante, with a request that he would continue the
work, which Dante consented to do.   In the *Compendio* there is practically no difference, except
that the *alcuno* has become *alcuno parente
di lui*.   In the Commentary, however (*Lez.* 33),
the story is given in much· fuller detail.   It is

narrated on the authority of Andrea Poggi,
Dante's sister's son, with whom Boccaccio was
intimate, and who himself related to him the
circumstances. In the confusion following Dante's
exile, and the plunder of his property, Gemma
had hurriedly stowed away several things of
value, including legal and other documents.
About five years later, when things were more
settled, she was advised to reclaim some of
Dante's property, and more particularly that
which formed part of her own dowry. She sent
Andrea Poggi with a lawyer (*procuratore*) to look
up such papers as were relevant to the case.
During their search they came upon the MS. of
Inferno, cantos I.-VII., as well as other poems of
Dante. They were submitted to Dino di messer
Lambertuccio, and the story then continues as
before. But Boccaccio adds that the same story
precisely (*puntualmente*) was told him by another
worthy man and citizen of Florence called Dino
Perini; the only difference in his narrative being
that he himself and not Andrea Poggi had
been the discoverer. Boccaccio professes himself
unable to decide between their rival claims; but
proceeds to point out a *prima facie* difficulty in
the story in any case, which he has never been
able satisfactorily to get over, viz. that these
cantos contain a definite prophecy by Ciacco of
an event happening *after* Dante's exile, viz. in
1304.[1] If so, they could not have been written

[1] The reference is to *Inf.* vi. 67.

before it, since Dante certainly had not the gift
of prophecy; and there is no evidence, remarks
Boccaccio, of any copy of these cantos in which
that passage does not occur. We shall point out
a little later the bearing of these details on the
question of the genuineness of the *Vita* and
Compendio, and their mutual relation.

Next (in Chapter xv.), we have the reasons for
the composition of the poem in Italian rather
than in Latin, the latter having been in fact the
earlier intention of the poet; and the first three
lines of the Latin draft are given, commencing

"Ultima regna canam fluido contermina mundo."

In his Commentary (*Lez.* i.), Boccaccio adds that
Dante had made some progress with the poem
before he abandoned the idea of writing it in
Latin. Two reasons are given for this change of
purpose in the *Vita*, the former of the two being
omitted both in the *Compendio* and the *Comento*.
The first was the desire to reach and to benefit
a wider circle of readers. The second was
this:—Dante observed that princes and great men,
who used to patronise and encourage poets, no
longer cared for liberal or philosophic pursuits,
and that Virgil and such like authors were either
neglected, or had passed into the hands of the
vulgar. Hence, in order to escape that fate, he
thought fit to adapt his own work, at least in
its external form,[1] to the tastes of the great men

[1] "Almeno nella corteccia di fuori" (*Comento*); "quanto
alla prima apparenza" (*Compendio*).

of the day, who, if they came across anything in
Latin, got it at once translated for them. Compare
what Dante says in *Convito* i. 10, as to his dread of
being translated by unskilful hands, warned by the
fate that had recently befallen Aristotle's *Ethics.*

After this we have the statement of the intended dedication of the three *Cantiche* of the
Commedia, "*a tre sollennissimi uomini italiani*";
the *Inferno* to Uguccione della Faggiuola; the
Purgatorio to Moruello Malaspina; the *Paradiso*
to Frederic III., king of Sicily. This was Frederic
of Arragon, commonly known as Frederic II., as
to whom we know that Dante's opinions under-
went a very great change shortly after the death of
Henry VII., so that before Dante completed the
Paradiso, he introduced several passages about
Frederic which prove that if he ever intended to
dedicate the work to him, he must have certainly
abandoned that intention, since Frederic would
have found much respecting himself not calculated
to recommend the work to his favour. He probably did so in any case, since he survived Dante
by about sixteen years. Boccaccio proceeds to
mention a different tradition, that Dante intended
to dedicate the whole to Can Grande, but he adds
in the *Vita* that there is no evidence on the point,
only arbitrary opinions; and that it is not a matter
worth serious investigation. The author of the
Compendio takes a different line, and definitely
professes his belief in the intended dedication of
the whole to Can Grande as more consonant

with the poet's habit, already mentioned, of sending him, before any one else, a few cantos from time to time, as soon as they were ready.

Chapter XVI. treats of the composition of the other works of Dante.   First, the *De Monarchia* is said to have been composed on the occasion of the descent of the Emperor Henry VII. into Italy. This is on many grounds improbable.   The decision of the date of this work is still a matter of the liveliest dispute, and the statement of Boccaccio looks suspiciously like an *a priori* guess from quite general and superficial considerations of suitability.   We are next told how the *De Monarchia* was condemned and publicly burnt at Bologna by the Cardinal Bertrand de Poyet (Beltrando del Poggetto), Papal Legate in Lombardy a few years after the poet's death, and that, but for the opposition of Pino della Tosa, the cardinal would have condemned his own memory to eternal infamy and confusion by burning at the same time the bones of Dante himself.   So we read in the *Vita*, but for this sentiment is substituted in the *Compendio* the very strange and cautious remark, *se giustamente o no, Iddio il sa !*—words which surely no one could seriously suppose Boccaccio to have written.   Next we have an account of the *Ecloghe*, the *Convito*, and, *già vicino alla sua morte*, the *De Vulgari Eloquio*,[1] and finally (in the *Vita*, but not in the *Compendio*) the *Epistles* and the *Canzoniere* are mentioned.

[1] I have retained the usual form *Eloquio*.   Boccaccio writes *Eloquentia*.   So also Lionardo (*inf.* p. 80).

In these two chapters we see that Boccaccio professes to give an account of the order of composition of Dante's principal works. It should be observed that a person writing some forty years or more after their appearance had scarcely any better means of forming an opinion on such a point than we have. There was no such thing as formal publication to go by, and the question then, as now, would have to be determined chiefly by a minute study of internal evidence. It need hardly be said that in the possession and application of criticism of this sort the advantage is entirely on the side of the moderns. Indeed, we cannot but suspect that we can trace throughout the superficial and *prima facie* grounds on which Boccaccio based his offhand conclusions. As to the *Vita Nuova*, there could of course be little room for doubt that it was the earliest work. That the *Convito* in a general way followed it, also seems naturally pointed out by the well-known passage in which Dante refers to it as carrying on in a more mature spirit the subject of the *Vita Nuova*; though a careful study of the several *Trattati* makes it very probable that they were composed at periods separated by some interval of time, very difficult to determine with any precision. It was obvious too to suggest, as Boccaccio does, that the *Commedia* was commenced in 1300, from a plausible and superficial interpretation of *Inf.* i. 1, though it involves (as I have already noticed) an entirely unauthorised identification of the date poetically assumed for the Vision with the actual date of the commencement of its composition. Then again, it was natural to associate the composition of the *De Monarchia* with the advent of the Emperor Henry VII. to Italy, and the brilliant hopes of the poet inspired by that event. Here again the study of the internal evidence makes the date of the work a matter of extreme doubt, as I have already observed. Finally, it was obvious to say that the *De Vulgari Eloquio* was written *vicino alla sua morte*, because it is an unfinished fragment.[1] We need not necessarily therefore accept all that Boccaccio says here, because we believe that we have materials and opportunities as good as, or better than, his for forming a judgment. But this does not affect his *bona fides*, or his trustworthiness, as to the many other points narrated by him, on which he certainly had ample and excellent means for obtaining information.

The chapter ends with an eloquent contrast between a life spent on such works as these, and the foolish, even when not wicked, pursuits which occupy the lives and the thoughts of most men.

The concluding chapter (with unimportant differences in the two narratives) relates and expounds at inordinate length a fabulous dream by which there was vouchsafed to the mother of Dante, shortly before his birth, a prophetic intimation of his future greatness and destiny.

---

[1] The most probable date would seem to be 1305-7. (See Fraticelli's Introduction.)

We are now in a position to discuss the probable authorship of these two forms of the Life which bear Boccaccio's name and their relation to one another; and after that to make some estimate of the value and authority of the record which has thus been transmitted to us.

I have no doubt whatever myself that the *Vita*, and that alone, is the genuine work of Boccaccio, and that the *Compendio* is an unauthorised revision by some later hand. The arguments by which I should support this view are as follows :—

First, I should maintain that only *one* of these works—leaving aside at present the question *which* it was—could have proceeded from the pen of Boccaccio.

(i) The language in which he himself, in the first Lecture of his Commentary, refers to a *trattatello in lode di Dante*, written by himself, for further information as to the poet's life, etc., seems to exclude the possibility of two forms of the work *then* existing. It is scarcely possible that an author who had (*ex hypothesi*) lately remodelled his own work, introducing changes of such magnitude and importance, should not have noticed the fact when making such a reference. After taking so much trouble he would surely wish that the revised work should replace the other. Of course this leaves open the question of a revision later still, but as this Lecture was delivered in October 1373, and Boccaccio died in December 1375, the available period is a short one, and the considerations which follow reduce that period within still narrower limits.[1]

(ii) We are restricted then in any case to supposing that the re-writing of his Biography was undertaken by Boccaccio, if at all, during the last two years of his life, and while he was occupied with writing his Lectures or Commentary on the *Divina Commedia.* Now, in the first place, it is not likely that he would have undertaken such a task when his hands were so fully occupied with his new work, at which we know he laboured so continuously till his death that it breaks off suddenly in the middle of a Lecture, and even in the middle of a sentence.[2] But further, there are passages here and there in

[1] As to the time of the composition of the *Vita*, it has been assigned to dates varying from 1350 to 1364. The latest and more careful investigation of the internal evidence points to the last-named date, 1364.

[2] I do not know whether the death of Boccaccio was sudden or unexpected, but there is something pathetic about the abrupt termination of his *Comento* thus broken off in the middle of a sentence in the note upon *Inf.* xvii. 17. He has just described the excellence of the Tartar workmanship, and is apparently about to enter upon an account of the people themselves, for the last words of the Commentary are *Sono i Tartari . . . .* It is also noticeable that in the fourteenth, fifteenth, and sixteenth cantos he three or four times defers the consideration of the allegorical meaning in order that the whole subject may be treated once for all at the end of the seventeenth canto, *e.g.* vol. ii. pp. 389, 429, 455. We thus unfortunately miss some interesting points, and especially Boccaccio's explanation of the *corda* (xvi. 106), which he particularly promises to speak about (p. 455). [The pages here and elsewhere are those of Milanesi's Edition.]

these Lectures implying fuller knowledge, fresh researches, more mature opinions, on some subjects as compared with what we find in the Life or Lives. And the point to notice is this, that neither the *Vita* nor the *Compendio* shows any traces of these new lights. As he surely would have introduced them into such a revised edition as is supposed, one which is altered and often completely re-written in the freest manner, it seems that he cannot have undertaken such a revision either simultaneously with, or subsequently to, the introduction into the Commentary of this new matter on the subjects actually treated in the Life. As then the language of the first Lecture excludes the possibility of the supposed revision having been executed *previously* to the Commentary, so these passages almost prevent our supposing it to have been written afterwards. At any rate the available period is reduced to the time between the composition of Lecture I. and that of any subsequent Lecture in which such new lights are found; for if the revision were made later, the same new lights would have been introduced into it also. Further, unless we suppose these new lights to have been discovered only *immediately before* their being employed in the Commentary (which is not likely to have been always the case), the small limit of time in which such revision could possibly have taken place would be still further restricted.

I will give just two examples of this. One remarkable instance occurs in the thirty-third Lecture. As only sixty were completed at the time of his death, and the whole composition occupied little more than two years, we may put this Lecture at about the middle of the period, *i.e.* in the autumn of 1374. I have already explained (p. 30) the minute account there given of the discovery of the missing cantos of the *Inferno*, the disputed claim to the honour of that discovery, Boccaccio's inability to decide the question, and his interesting critical difficulties as to accepting the story at all. Of all this there is no trace either in the *Vita* or the *Compendio*, the former speaking of the discoverer vaguely as *alcuno* and the latter merely as *alcuno parente di lui*. Thus there would seem to be *at the most* only one year of Boccaccio's life left open at all for the alleged revision, and that the one probably the most fully occupied of all, when he was planning out his Commentary and writing the first portion of it.

Another argument of the same kind might be drawn from a comparison of the language about Attila " king of the Vandals " both in the *Vita* and the *Compendio* with the curious passage in the Commentary a little later (*Lez.* 47), on *Inf.* xii. 134,[1] where Boccaccio quotes Paulus Diaconus as his authority for the story of Attila and the sack of Florence (this latter event being more fully narrated by means of a definite citation from Giov. Villani on the Comment on xiii. 149).[2] Attila is there

---

[1] ii. p. 305. [2] ii. p. 355.

described as king of the Goths at the time of the Emperor Martian. He also observes that many persons called this Attila, Totila, but wrongly, since there was about ninety years between them. It seems likely that (as in the case mentioned above) the *Compendio*, if a revision by the author, would have had the benefit of this accession of knowledge (such as it is).[1]

(iii) The succeeding biographers, Villani, Lionardo, and Manetti, do not give a hint of any suspicion of there being two forms of Boccaccio's Life. Macrì-Leone appears to me to go too far when he says that these three writers know of the *Vita* only. It does not appear to me that in the case of the two former there is a particle of evidence in favour of their having used one form rather than the other, though in the case of Manetti it is different, as he quite distinctly had the *Vita* before him.[2] But this is anticipating a later step in the argument. As regards Lionardo, this fact has a special significance, since he wrote with the avowed object of criticising and supplementing the work of Boccaccio, which he says he had read most diligently, and more than once. He wrote his work in Florence itself, and about half a century after the death of Boccaccio, where if anywhere, and by which time if at all, the existence of Boccaccio's second work should have been known, and Lionardo, if any one, should have been aware of it.

[1] On the confusion of Attila and Totila, see Supplementary Notes. [2] See *inf.* p. 91.

In this way then I should claim to have established my *first* point, viz. that Boccaccio cannot be supposed to have written *both*, but *only one* of these works.   Next we ask, *which* is to be selected as the genuine one ?

The cumulative force of the following considerations seem to me to be conclusive in favour of the *Vita*.

(i) The genuineness of the *Vita* has approved itself to those critics who have gone into the question *almost unanimously*, whatever different opinions they may have held as to the claims of the *Compendio*.

(ii) The MSS. of the *Compendio* are not only fewer in number, but also much later in date than those of the *Vita*.   This statement I make on the authority of Macrì-Leone (p. lxvii), as I have had no opportunity of verifying it.

(iii) It is also mentioned by Macrì-Leone (p. xli) that in some MSS. of the *Compendio*, but in none of those of the *Vita*, we find not only the Epitaph of Giovanni del Virgilio (*Theologus Dantes*, etc.), the first which appeared on Dante's Tomb, but also those commencing *Jura Monarchie*, and *Inclita fama*.   The significance of this will appear from the discussion of the subject in my article on the tomb of Dante, printed in the *English Historical Review* for January 1889.

(iv) In Chapter V. of his Introduction Macrì-Leone has pointed out, by an elaborate series of comparisons between the *Comento* of Boccaccio and the two works we are considering, that Boccaccio himself throughout used the *Vita*, not the *Compendio*. We have (1) passages in the *Comento* corresponding closely with some of those in the *Vita* which are omitted in the *Compendio* ; (2) when passages occur in both works the language of the *Comento* much more nearly resembles that of the *Vita* than that of the *Compendio*, identical words and phrases peculiar to the former being often reproduced. It should further be observed that examples of this are drawn from all parts of the *Comento*, including some of the latest lectures. The same test is applied with the same result by the careful and laborious editor to other works of Boccaccio, such as the *Genealogia* and the *De' Casi degli Uomini Illustri* : *e.g.* in the latter we find the curious justificatory, or at least palliating, illustrations of licentiousness of life, from the examples of Hercules, Paris, David, Solomon, etc., which, it will be remembered, occur in Chapter XII. of the *Vita*, but are omitted in the *Compendio*.[1] Some examples of coincidences between the *Compendio* and the *Comento* have been alleged on the other side, but they are fewer and less striking, and can easily be explained by supposing that the author of the *Compendio* had access to the *Comento*.

(v) Next as to evidence of the same kind to

---

[1] If, however, the date of the *De' Casi*, etc., be *c.* 1362, or at any rate before 1364 (Macrì-Leone, p. lxxxix), this argument would be of no value. See *sup.* p. 38, note 1.

be derived from succeeding writers, I have already mentioned, and it will appear more clearly
later, that Manetti, writing nearly a century
afterwards, and copying, as he does most freely,
though (as then usual) without acknowledgment,
from Boccaccio, frequently borrows the very
language of the *Vita*, but betrays no similar
knowledge of any of the characteristic passages
of the *Compendio*, nor does he appear to be aware
of the existence of any second form of the work.
To this may be added the fact that Benvenuto
da Imola, who at Bologna followed Boccaccio
as Lecturer on Dante, in his Commentary on
Purg. xxx. 31 (vol. iv. pp. 210-11) copies very
closely (though again without acknowledgment)
several statements and phrases straight from
Boccaccio's account of the first meeting of Dante
and Beatrice Portinari, and it is quite clear
that he quoted from the *Vita*, not the *Compendio*, since many, and some of the most
striking, of the expressions are peculiar to the
former.

How then should we account for the fact that
this supposed revision by the author was so far
from supplanting the original work that it was
unknown to all succeeding writers whose special
business it was to be acquainted with it, and (as
argued above) that the MSS. in which it exists
are both fewer in number and of much later date
than those of the *Vita*, which *ex hypothesi* it was
so very early intended to replace?

(vi) Another very suspicious circumstance is found in the existence of at least three other forms of *Compendio* or *rifacimento* of the *Vita*, besides several Latin paraphrases, résumés, and selections, varying more or less from the original work (Macrì-Leone, p. lxvii). The inference from this would be that the practice was not by any means uncommon, and that the Life by Boccaccio was regarded as a sort of common property of authors, a kind of public quarry from which any one might take what he liked, and use it as he pleased. Nor is such treatment peculiar to this work only. Such a habit of plagiarism was then not at all unusual, a wholly different standard of public opinion evidently existing on the subject, due perhaps partly to the much smaller chance of detection, when works were not formally published, and existed only in MSS. ; and partly perhaps to the absence of troublesome reviewers with inconvenient memories. We have a remarkable instance of this practice in the case of the early Commentaries on Dante. Not only are whole notes repeated bodily and *verbatim,* but sometimes even whole pages with little or no variation. The most extraordinary case is that of the Commentary known as the *Anonimo Fiorentino,* where the whole of the notes on the *Paradiso,* and about two-thirds of those on the *Purgatorio,* are a simple reproduction, without any acknowledgment, of the older Commentary of Jacopo della Lana. We often find in attempting to con-

struct a *catena* of the old Commentaries on some
particular passage, that they are πολλῶν ὀνομά-
των μορφὴ μία.

(vii) I have also already noted that some of
the details added in the *Compendio* are such that,
if known to Boccaccio at all, they are not likely to
have first become known to him late in his life, and
moreover there was full occasion for his introducing them into his first draft of the work, if he
knew them.   Further, they have just the appearance of the kind of gossip by which a simple
narrative always has a tendency to be overlaid in
the process of time, while on the other hand there
is a singular absence of any fresh information such
as the author might be expected to have gathered,
and such as we know from his Commentary he
actually did gather upon some points.   Under
this head we may notice a very curious contra-
diction on a fundamental point as we may call it,
which occurs in the two works in respect of the
effect of Dante's love for Beatrice on his work and
genius.   In the *Vita* (c. iii.) it is argued that if that
passion could interfere with appetite, sleep, and
mental repose, *a fortiori* it would be a sore impediment *ai sacri studi e allo ingegno*.   He adds
that he lays stress upon this because some have
asserted that it was a stimulus, not an impediment,
judging from graceful works in verse in praise of
the object of his love, which certainly are not to
be ranked as the highest efforts of art.   Certainly
he adds, " I do not agree to this " (*Ma certo io nol*

consento). It is very curious to set in contrast
with this emphatic expression of opinion the
language of the corresponding passage of the
Compendio : " By the sight of her was first aroused
in him the feeling that he must compose in poetry
. . . and such a master of this art did he become under the stimulus of love that he far
surpassed the fame of all previous poets, and
many think that he will never be surpassed in
the future." Now this fundamental divergence
of opinion on such a subject as this looks more
like the views of two different men than the
opinions of the same man at different times.
Had any one (which is very unlikely) seen reason
thus to change an opinion that he had before so
positively asserted as against those who thought
otherwise, and actually in the same context, he
would surely have drawn attention to its being
a recantation.

(viii) The minor changes, such as the alterations
of single words and phrases, seem to me clearly
to point to the *Vita* being the *original* work, and
if so, the only genuine one, since we cannot attribute both to Boccaccio. The following are some
illustrations of this : (*a*) The rather singular
word *partitamente* occurs twice in the *Vita,* in the
sense of " in detail." In Chapter III. (*sub init.*) it is
changed in the *Compendio* into *più distesamente,*
and in Chapter v. (*sub fin.*) it disappears in the
altered form of the sentence. To say nothing of
the latter case, the substitution in the former looks

like the introduction of a more familiar expression, and the *lectio facilior* is likely to have been the later form. (β) The cautious omission in the *Compendio* of the name Alberto della Scala in Chapter v. and the substitution of the vague phrase *il signore della terra* is probably due to the doubt as to the identification of the *gran Lombardo* of *Paradiso* xvii. 71 (on which passage this statement is probably founded). The reviser, being aware of this difficulty, thought it safer to leave the matter open. (γ) The hyperbole at the end of Chapter v. in the *Vita, io direi, che egli fosse in terra divenuto un Iddio*, appears in the *Compendio* in the milder form *che . . . sia di doppia corona da onorare*. The exaggerated language of enthusiasm gives place to the well-measured phrase of cool reflection. The reverse process would be very much less likely.

(ix) There is a considerable insertion in Chapter x. in the *Compendio* introduced by the words, "I could now perhaps go on to another point if some senseless persons had not drawn me back again for a little space to this argument". It certainly seems more reasonable to regard this as an addition to the original draft of the passage, than to regard its non-appearance as an omission.[1]

As a supplement to these considerations I would point out the extreme weakness of the positive arguments by which the authorship of Boccaccio

---

[1] For another similar argument, see *sup.* p. 10, note 1.

is claimed for the *Compendio*. At the very most they show that it is not impossible or quite inconceivable that he should have revised his work in this manner. As far as I know, the principal arguments are three.

(i) The evident tendency to mitigate the severity of the language used about Florence. This, it is urged, would be natural in Boccaccio, since he was appointed by the people of Florence to lecture on Dante, and employed as their representative to convey a subsidy to Dante's daughter Beatrice, and in some other public matters. True enough; but since the author, whoever he may have been, was a citizen of Florence, as he several times asserts, the *carità del natio loco* would supply an adequate motive for his manipulation of the work in this manner. It should also be stated that in the *Comento, i.e.* Lectures actually delivered in Florence itself by Boccaccio, he is not deterred from speaking out in the very strongest language about the conduct of his fellow-citizens toward Dante. So again in his *Lez.* 22 he scourges the vices of Florentine society in language rivalling that of Juvenal both in its severity and also in its outspokenness. And in *Lez.* 31 (ii. p. 115) he gives the Tuscans, and *in singolarità* the Florentines, as examples of the curse (*maledizione*) of ungovernable and irreconcilable anger. Also he justifies very unreservedly the accusation of Dante in *Inf.* xv. 16, *Gent' è avara, invidiosa, e superba* (ii. p. 415).

(ii) It is alleged that the *Compendio* is distinguished by its more pronounced orthodoxy and
the greater fervency of its Catholic sentiments,
and that this accords with the religious character
of Boccaccio's later years.   I confess I have not
been able to trace this difference between the
two works with any clearness,[1] excepting perhaps
in the very curious saving clause already quoted
(p. 34) as to the conduct of the Papal Legate,
who purposed burning the bones of Dante; but,
granting that it exists, it only implies a state of
mind in the author which was too common to
lead to his identification.   The reformed Boccaccio
may have been ever so good a Catholic, but he
was not the only one in Florence "among the
Christians of the fourteenth century", to borrow
Dante's expression on the *Vita Nuova*.

(iii) Another reason suggested is a general desire
to abbreviate the original work.   But in the first
place, in the Commentary, *Lez.* 1, Boccaccio speaks
of it as being merely a *trattatello*, and so not likely
to require an abridgment; in the next place the
Compendio often expands the original, and the
total result is not, I think, a very marked
difference of length, certainly very little indeed,
if we except the reduction effected by omitting
(for a special reason unconnected with brevity)
the long and repeated denunciations of Florence.

---

[1] At the end of Chap. IV., for instance, a fervent religious
exhortation to "set one's affections on things above" occurs
in the *Vita* only, and not in the *Compendio*.

Finally, if abbreviation were the motive, it surely does not follow, when any document, a sermon, for instance, or a lecture, is too long, that the only person conscious of this or desiring to curtail it is the author himself.

Having thus (as it appears to me) convinced ourselves of the genuineness of the *Vita* of Boccaccio, and also that we probably need not concern ourselves further with any other form of it than that usually received, let us endeavour in conclusion to estimate its value and authority.

Now the credibility of such a work depends on two things : (1) the opportunities for information possessed by its author; and (2) the character of the author himself. We will take them in order, and as to the first we further note that the opportunities for information are of two kinds, general and special.

In a general sense, any one whatever living either as a contemporary with, or very soon after, the events or persons about which or whom he writes, has obviously opportunities both for gathering, and also for testing, information such as no later author can possess. This qualification of course Boccaccio, as we have already observed, possessed in a pre-eminent degree.

But he had also *special* qualifications from his actual intercourse with friends and relations of the poet himself. Not only was he brought into contact, as we have seen, with Dante's own daughter Beatrice, but there are three other

persons mentioned by Boccaccio by name, either
relations or intimate friends of Dante himself,
from whom he expressly says that he received
definite information. First we have Pier Giardino
of Ravenna, who, as we read near the beginning
of Boccaccio's Commentary,[1] was one of the most
intimate and devoted friends whom Dante had in
Ravenna. Now Pier Giardino himself informed
Boccaccio of Dante's age as it was stated to him
by Dante when he lay upon his deathbed. Pier
is again mentioned in the *Vita* (c. XIV.), where
he is described as *lungamente stato discepolo di
Dante*, as the authority for Boccaccio's statement
of the strange loss and recovery of the last thirteen
cantos of the *Paradiso*. Pier Giardino had no
doubt the incident well impressed on his memory

> "chiavata in mezzo della testa
> Con maggior chiovi, che d'altrui sermone," [2]

by the fact that he was knocked up out of his bed
one night before daybreak by Dante's son Jacopo,
who came] to tell him of the mysterious vision
which he had had during the night in reference to
the lost cantos. Now recent researches have discovered abundant contemporary documents proving the presence of Pier Giardino at Ravenna
early in the fourteenth century, and notably in
the years 1320, 1328, 1346, etc. (See Guerrini e
Ricci, *Studi e Polemiche Dantesche.*) Further,
besides other documentary evidence of the pre-

[1] *Lez.* 2, vol. i. p. 104.   [2] *Purg.* viii. 137-8.

sence of Boccaccio also at Ravenna, we have an extract from the *Storie Ravennati* of Rossi, given by Guerrini, etc., pp. 38-9 : *Joannes Boccatius . . . frequenter consueverat urbem hanc, ubi Boccatiorum familia Ravennas erat.*

Next we have Dante's nephew, son of his sister, by name Andrea Poggi. In the Commentary on *Inf.* viii. 1, he is mentioned as having narrated to Boccaccio, with whom he was intimate (*dimestico divenuto*),[1] the story of the loss and recovery of *Inf.* Cantos I.-VII., claiming to have been himself the person who discovered them. Boccaccio there describes this Andrea Poggi as marvellously resembling Dante in face and stature, and moreover that he walked as though he were slightly humpbacked, as Dante himself is said to have done (*come Dante si dice che faceva*). After testifying to his straightforward and honest character, Boccaccio states that he knew him intimately, and that he derived much information from him respecting Dante's ways and habits (*costumi e modi*).

We have yet a third person mentioned by name with whom Boccaccio had communications on the subject of Dante, viz. Dino Perini, the rival claimant (as already mentioned) for the discovery of the missing cantos. He narrated the story himself to Boccaccio, and he had enjoyed (as Boccaccio adds) according to his own statement, the greatest possible intimacy and friendship with

[1] *Lez.* 33, ii. p. 129.

Dante (*stato quanto più esser si potesse familiare ed amico di Dante*).[1]

Again, in his Commentary on *Inf.* ii. 57, *Lez.* 8 (vol. i. p. 224), Boccaccio says that his information about Beatrice Portinari (and this is important, as our knowledge of her rests on his statement alone) was derived by him from the mouth of a person worthy of trust, who not only knew her, but was very closely connected with her (*fu per consanguinità strettissima a lei*).

Here then we have five or six distinct sources of direct and special information both accessible to and actually employed by Boccaccio, besides the opportunities for general information possessed by any intelligent person living at a time so very nearly contemporary with the subject of his narrative.

This being so, let us pass on to the other and last point. Seeing that the writer *could* give us trustworthy information, is there any reason to doubt that he *did* do so? Have we any ground for suspecting in the author himself, either deliberate perversion of the truth, or the incapacity, from want of sober judgment or the critical faculty, to keep himself within its limits?

---

[1] Two other cases may be added from the *Comento*. (1) In *Lez.* 58 (ii. p. 434) his account of Gualdrada is given :— *secondochè soleva il venerabile uomo Coppo di Borghese Domenichi raccontare, al quale per certo furono le notabili cose della nostra città notissime.* (2) His explanation of *Inf.* xvi. 100 is derived from information which he received from the Abbot of the Monastery, while he was himself on a visit there (ii. p. 451).

It has often been maintained that this was the case with Boccaccio. Lionardo (whose Life we shall consider later) regards that of Boccaccio as a tissue of fables and gossip. And quite recently so sober a critic as Scartazzini (quoted by Witte, *Dante-Forschungen*, ii. p. 54)[1] declares with much emphasis that in this work Boccaccio has "written a poem or a romance, not a history".

Now such criticism as this appears to me to proceed on a very false and superficial notion of the conditions and limits of trustworthiness in any author, and especially in one living in a different age, and trained in different habits of thought from our own. No doubt the author of the *Decameron* is to be credited with a lively imagination, and a keen sense of dramatic effect; but are these conditions, which naturally have full play when the author is professedly composing fiction or poetry, entirely incompatible with veracity (subject of course to the different conceptions of accuracy, and of the value of evidence in the fourteenth and nineteenth centuries), when he undertakes to write history?[2]

Is it quite impossible to suppose that, as the "spirits of the prophets are subject to the prophets", so even a poet may exercise some control over his imagination when he sets himself to deal with facts? Doubtless these qualities in

---

[1] A similarly unfavourable judgment is even more emphatically repeated by Scartazzini in his *Vita di Dante* in the *Manuali Hoepli*, p. 6. Prof. Bartoli adopts, though with some modifications, the view of Scartazzini. See *Storia della Lett. Ital.*, v. p. 310.   [2] See Supplementary Notes.

Boccaccio may have coloured and heightened some of his pictures, but we have no reason therefore to suppose that he has entirely falsified or invented them. We may well give up, for example, such mythical elements as the dream of Dante's mother, and also perhaps that of his son Jacopo, as due to the superstition or facile credulity of the age. But that is no reason for denying that some portions of the poem were probably lost, and strangely and unexpectedly recovered. We may well believe this without necessarily accepting the element of the marvellous with which fancy has surrounded the surprising fact of their recovery. That such facts should be thus clothed with accessories of mystery is as much a result of the age in which they were recorded, as that the movements of the heavenly bodies should be described in the language of the cycles and epicycles of the Ptolemaic system. Or to take another point. We need not accept Boccaccio's offhand and positive assertion as to the dates of Dante's several works, since, as we have seen, the superficial reasons for some of his statements are not difficult to guess, and the actual determination of this complicated question is one depending on minute and careful criticism, which is certainly not to be looked for in the age when he wrote, and assuredly is not found even in Dante himself. But the rejection of such portions of the work as these, and perhaps even much else, is no reason whatever for casting doubt upon those others in which Boccaccio had unique and copious opportunities for securing knowledge, and as to which there is simply no reason whatever for saying what is false, rather than what is true; I mean such details—and most interesting they are—as the features, gait, habits, manners, and other personal traits of the poet, which I hope to gather together in a later part of this work. Here there is simply no motive for invention or falsification, for it is by no means an ideal picture, and these details were still fresh and lively in the minds and memories of many with whom Boccaccio had familiar intercourse. As Dr. Witte very well remarks, "though we find much that we reject as fabulous in the history of Livy, and that even in the later periods of his narrative as well as the earlier, we do not therefore feel any suspicion as to the truthfulness of his account of the Second Punic War". Even so, I feel no doubt that in the Life of Boccaccio, though we may not commit ourselves to the accuracy of every fact and detail, we certainly have a generally trustworthy and truthful picture of Dante as he appeared to his contemporaries, and as he lived in the memories of his fellow-men.

Most grateful should we be to Boccaccio for this precious heritage; for not only is it recorded in his own delicious and inimitable prose, not only is the portrait traced with a loving and skilful hand, but without it we should not have possessed any such portraiture at all.

CHAPTER III.

THE LIFE BY FILIPPO VILLANI.

THE next biography we meet with is that of
Filippo Villani in his *Liber de Civitatis Flor-
entinæ Famosis Civibus*. Filippo Villani came
of a family of chroniclers, and was nephew of the
more celebrated Giovanni of that name. His
Lives (between thirty and forty in number) are
written in Latin, and they are mostly very meagre
and slight, often only a few lines, that of Dante
being much the longest, though not occupying
many pages. It follows that of Claudian, which
begins the series. There were no poets, he says,
worth recording between, for with Claudian
ancient poetry seemed to die, and Dante was the
first to wake her from her long and death-like
sleep. The life is strangely entitled *De vita
et moribus Dantis insignis comici*[1]—" The life
and character of Dante, the distinguished com-
edian ". Alas! poor Dante! Our hopes are not

---

[1] He speaks of Dante elsewhere as *Comicus noster Dantes.*
Three of his heroes are rather ambiguously described as
Semipoetae, though by this he merely means to indicate that
they had some other claim to distinction as well.

raised high by such an exordium, *tanto hiatu* as Horace says. In truth the life is a very meagre one; it tells us little or nothing new, and is scarcely more than a *réchauffé* of that of Boccaccio, to which the writer refers us for further information. The cause of the decay of poetry, according to Villani, was the discouragement by the authorities of Christendom of heathen poetry as being nothing but mischievous folly. But Dante not only showed how poetry could be made subservient to Christian doctrine, but also pointed out that the Holy Spirit had overruled the utterances of even the heathen poets, when rightly understood, to foreshadow Christian truth. Villani next gives an account of the poet's family and ancestry resembling that of Boccaccio, but as his authority for it states, *a majoribus gentis meae, qui scribendo rei gestae dederunt operam, me memini audisse*; referring, no doubt, to his distinguished father and uncle, Matteo and Giovanni Villani.

The ultimate origin of the family he traces (with Boccaccio) to Rome, and in particular to Eliseo of the noble family of Frangipani, so called because they "broke bread" in distribution from their own granaries to the starving people on the occasion of a great famine. After the family had been settled for many generations at Florence there arose Cacciaguida, who married a wife from the noble stock of the Adiguerii (so he writes the name) of Parma, correcting the statement, found

(as it will be remembered) in Boccaccio, that
the Ferrara was the origin of the race.   This
he attributes to *modernus quidam* actuated by a
desire to flatter the family of Este.[1]   The name of
the family was next spelt Aldighieri and then
Allaghieri, which form Villani says was that
finally adopted.   After some mythical details
about his infancy and childhood—*e.g.* that even
as a baby he was so serious that he repelled the
vanity of his mother's kisses (*dum pueritiae dies
in matris gremio . . . morosius observaret, asper-
nareturque fallentia matris oscula!*), and as a boy
he walked (very unlike other boys) *gravi atque
librato incessu*.   We are informed that he studied
theology at Paris, and in disputations displayed
an astonishing power of memory.   At first sight
it might seem that Villani placed the visit to
Paris (like Serravalle) in Dante's youth; but the
context shows that he is mentioning it out of
its proper order.   In connection with Dante's
devotion to poetry, Villani goes back to explain
that his boyish and perfectly pure love for
Beatrice (*amore castissimo qui in ipso pueritiae
limine coepit*) incited him to compose *multas
morales cantilenas*, which were brought together
by himself into one work entitled *Vita Nuova*.
But after her death he began the more arduous
task of the *Divina Commedia*, which, however,
was interrupted, after the completion of seven
cantos, by his exile.   It is curious to observe

[1] See Supplementary Notes.

that Villani considers the main cause of Dante's
exile to have been the odium caused in many
quarters by the haughty speech which he is said
to have uttered on the occasion of his appoint-
ment to conduct an embassy to Pope Boniface:
"If I go, who remains? if I remain, who goes?"
Villani then relates at some length the story of
the loss and discovery of the first seven cantos,
or "Odes" as he calls them, of the *Inferno*,
but without mentioning the name of the discoverer. (See what was said about this under
Boccaccio.)

We have a detailed account (and this is the
most interesting and original feature in the work,
since of this there is nothing in Boccaccio) of the
occasion of the poet's last illness. He was sent
by his patron Guido Novello da Polenta on an
embassy to Venice, but the Venetians, dreading
(says Villani) the power of his eloquence, re-
peatedly refused to grant him an audience. At
last, being sick with fever (*laborans febribus*),
he begged them to convey him back to Ravenna
by sea; but they, increasing in their fury against
him (*majori laborantes insania*), utterly refused
this, so that he had to undertake the fatiguing
and unhealthy journey by land. This so aggra-
vated the fever from which he was suffering that
he died a few days after his arrival at Ravenna.
We have some details about his burial, especially that *apud vestibulum Fratrum Minorum
eminenti conditus est sepulcro.* The difficulty of

giving an exact meaning to this and similar expressions has been explained in my article on the Tomb of Dante already referred to (*sup.* p. 23), where also I have noticed the apparent inaccuracy of Villani's statement that Guido Novello ordered the epitaph of Giovanni del Virgilio (*Theologus Dantes*, etc.) to be inscribed on the tomb.[1] Minute details follow as to Dante's appearance, habits, and character, which I reserve (as in the case of Boccaccio and the other biographers) to be gathered together in one view later on. I will only notice one point here, which stands in remarkable contrast with the celebrated remark of Boccaccio as to the *ampissimo loco* which *lussuria* had in Dante, and the still more offensive amplification of this charge in the *Compendio*. Villani says that he was *vitae continentissimæ, cibi potusque parcissimus.*

The Life ends with a fervid eulogium of the *Commedia*, which not unworthily he thinks might be described as *felicis vitæ speculum*, and with many expressions of admiration of the firm resolution of the poet in labouring on for twenty-three years at this noble work, undeterred by suffering, exile, poverty, the patronage of the great, and many other troubles and obstacles, so that only he might benefit his fellow-citizens and the world at large, by recalling, through the means of his terrible satire, those who were walking in dark-

---

[1] "Hos (versus) qui fuere Magistri Joannis de Virgilio jussit in frontispicio solemnis arculae insigniri."

ness to the paths of light.[1] It is to be observed
that there is here not the slightest allusion to any
domestic troubles or difficulties, which formed
such a prominent feature in the corresponding
passages of Boccaccio's Life. The panegyric concludes with the expression, elsewhere assigned
with some amplification to Petrarch, that no one
could have written a work at once so sublime and
so profound without the special aid of the Holy
Spirit. Villani then describes at some length
the vision vouchsafed to Jacopo by which his
father indicated to him where the missing
cantos (*odas plerasque*, the number not specified)
of the *Paradiso* were found. By this miracle
(says Villani) the divine character of the poet's
work is clearly established. It is curious that
after thus swallowing the camel he strains out
the gnat of the dream of the mother of Dante.
This he peremptorily dismisses as fabulous,
though narrated by Boccaccio, to whom in conclusion he refers his readers for fuller information as to the details of Dante's life, of which he
says Boccaccio's work may be almost described
as "a diary" (*ubi propemodum ephemeridas ejus
explicuit*). It will be observed that this Life
gives us very little, except the story of the
Venetian Embassy, that was not already found
more fully in the Life of Boccaccio.

[1] Compare Dante's own language in *Conv.* i. 1.

CHAPTER IV.

THE LIFE BY LIONARDO BRUNI (COMMONLY CALLED LIONARDO ARETINO).

A MUCH more original character and critical value belongs to the next of the Early Biographies which we have to consider, that of Lionardo Bruni,[1] commonly known from the name of his birthplace as Lionardo Aretino. Born in 1369 and dying in 1444, he was thus a little more than a century later than Dante, and about half a century later than Boccaccio. He was well acquainted with both Latin and Greek literature, and translated several Greek works, parts of Aristotle, Plato, Demosthenes, etc., and was able to address a Greek oration to the Greek Emperor and Patriarch at the Council of Constance. He filled important political posts at Rome and at Florence, and, regarding him as a biographer of Dante, it is interesting to note that

---

[1] This Life has been several times printed. It is included (together with the Lives of Dante by F. Villani and Manetti) in the collection published by Mazzoni, Florence, 1847. It is also found in the following editions of the *Divina Commedia* :—Poggiali 1807 ; Venturi 1821 ; Brunone Bianchi 1857, and in some others.

he was at the Council of Constance in attendance
on Pope John XXIII., at which Council there was
also present John of Serravalle, who, at the instance of the two English Bishops, Hallam and
Bubwith (also present at the Council), wrote a
Commentary on the *Commedia,* including a brief
biography of its author, the chief interest of which
is the novel and unsupported assertion already
referred to of Dante's visit to England, and to
London and Oxford in particular. Lionardo, who,
as we shall presently see, is entirely ignorant of
any such journey, and by implication excludes
the possibility of it, must doubtless have met
Serravalle and his patrons at the Council. It is
curious to speculate whether they compared notes
or otherwise discoursed together about the subject of their common literary labours. Lionardo
was a somewhat voluminous writer on a variety of subjects, some of his works being in
Latin and some in Italian. His chief work is
a *Historia Florentina* from the earliest times to
1404.

In the particular work with which we are
concerned he begins by taking his readers into
his confidence in a very pleasant and lively
manner. " I had just completed," he says, " a few
days ago a somewhat laborious work,[1] and I
felt the want of some literary recreation, for

[1] Probably he is referring to some of his labours on Aristotle, about which a good deal is to be found in his *Familiar
Letters.*

E

variation in the subjects of study is quite as
necessary as variety in one's diet. Just as I was
thinking about this, I chanced to take up again
the life of Dante by Boccaccio, a book which I
had indeed formerly read with much care. It
struck me that Boccaccio, excellent man and
charming writer though he is, had written the
life of the sublime poet as though he had
been undertaking another Filocolo, Filostrato or
Fiammetta (referring to well-known light works
of Boccaccio). Indeed he seems to write with
the idea that a man is born into the world for
nothing else but to qualify himself for a place
in the *Decameron.* Consequently, Boccaccio has
recorded numerous trivialities about the life of
Dante, but has neglected the weightier and more
serious parts of his life (*ricordando le cose leggieri
e tacendo le gravi*). This omission Lionardo pro-
poses to supply, and he wishes his work to be
regarded as supplementary rather than antagon-
istic to that of Boccaccio "—*con maggior notizia
delle cose stimabili.*

First we have the usual details as to Dante's
ancestry, though Lionardo cautiously warns us
that all that professes to go further back than
his *tritavo* Cacciaguida is, in his opinion, mere
guess-work. He gives a minute account of the
situation in Florence of the houses occupied by
the Elisei and the Aldighieri (so spelt, as in
Boccaccio, etc.); the modern orthography being
given in the form Alleghieri. The future poet

was born in 1265, after the return of the Guelfs,
who had been exiled after the defeat of Mont'
Aperti. (Every one will remember the splendid
episode of Farinata in *Inf.* x., where this great
battle in 1260 and its consequences are referred
to.) In reference to the return of the Guelfs, it
seems that Lionardo is indulging in a little
a priori history. He, I suppose, thought it
necessary to get them back before 1265 in order
to account for Dante's birth in Florence. As a
matter of fact, they did not return till the year
1267, after the overthrow of Manfred by Charles
of Anjou in the fatal battle of Benevento. (See
Purg. iii.) It is generally supposed that for
some reason or other Dante's father must either
have escaped the banishment, or have returned
from it earlier than the main body of the exiles.
His father died when Dante was still a boy, but
under the care of Brunetto Latini he devoted
himself with the utmost diligence to all liberal
studies, not however withdrawing himself from
the society of his fellows, so that he even arrived
at some distinction in the practice of arms.
Dante had an early opportunity for displaying
his prowess in this respect, for at the age of
twenty-four he fought in the important and
memorable battle of Campaldino. Of this battle
Lionardo gives a minute and interesting account.
Dante was fighting on horseback in the very
front of the battle,[1] and very narrowly indeed

[1] Lionardo's words are — *combattendo vigorosamente a*

escaped with his life, for in this part of the battle the Aretines were successful, and the Florentine cavalry was disastrously routed. An interesting statement is here made by Lionardo: " This battle Dante describes in one of his letters, and says that he himself fought in it, and he also draws a plan of the battle ". This may or may not have been in some part of the letter quoted a few pages later; but in the passage there reproduced by Lionardo, Dante says little more than that he was in very great fear, *ebbi temenza molta*. We wonder very much how he comported himself. Were his military reminiscences perhaps something like those of Horace—

> " celerem fugam
> Sensi, relicta non bene parmula " ?

little round shield

Another reflection, too, cannot but occur. We can scarcely think, without a shudder, on what is implied by the simple words of the biographer, *portò gravissimo pericolo*. Little did those Aretine horsemen know what a light might then have been quenched by some chance blow from a nameless hand.

cavallo nella prima schiera. If so, may not the following lines perhaps describe a personal reminiscence ?

> "Qual esce alcuna volta di galoppo
> Lo cavalier di schiera, che cavalchi
> E va per farsi onor del primo intoppo."
> *Purg.* xxiv. 94-6.

So also *Purg.* xxxii. 19-24 looks like a reminiscence of Dante's military experience. More direct references are found in *Inf.* xxi. 94 ; xxii. 1-9. Add *Purg.* v. 91, etc.

Lionardo regrets that Boccaccio did not record Dante's courage and patriotism at Campaldino rather than his nine-years-old love *e simili leggierezze*; quoting rather cruelly two characteristically neat Italian proverbs to illustrate the preference here shown by Boccaccio—*La lingua pur va dove il dente duole; e a cui piace il bere, sempre ragiona di vini.* So completely does Lionardo himself eschew any such *leggierezze,* that he never mentions Dante's meeting with or devotion to Beatrice at all, which certainly, whether in itself a *leggierezza* or not, was the turning-point of his whole life, nor does the name of Beatrice so much as once occur throughout the whole of the Life of Lionardo!

After this Dante returned home and devoted himself with redoubled assiduity to study ; but so thoroughly (Lionardo is careful to tell us) did he enjoy all the social pleasures of life that no one would have supposed that he was a student. On this Lionardo remarks that he never knew a real student or one of true genius who did not do the same, nor any unsociable recluse—*questi camuffati,* as he contemptuously calls them — who ever knew three letters. *L'ingegno grande ed alto non ha bisogno di tali tormenti!* "If a man does not learn quickly, he will never learn at all; so that to shut one's-self up and avoid society is entirely confined to those whose dull intellect is utterly unfit for any learning whatever." Every one, I suppose, has his own special object of dislike. The bugbear of Boccaccio was the female sex; we begin to perceive that the pet aversion of Lionardo was what would now, I suppose, be called (if I may venture on the expression) "a smug". He is most careful to defend his hero on every occasion against such a suspicion.

Next he points out that Dante showed his sociable disposition also by taking to himself a wife in his youth. Boccaccio (he says) quite loses his temper over this, and declares that wives are enemies to study. Does he forget that Socrates, the noblest philosopher that ever lived, had a wife? (Lionardo surely here chose rather an unfortunate example for his purpose.) And that Aristotle too, whose wisdom could not be surpassed, had two wives—at different times (as Lionardo is careful to add)—to say nothing of examples of Roman philosophers and statesmen, such as Cicero, Cato, Seneca, and Varro. Moreover, *pace* Boccaccio again, man is a social animal (*animal civile*), as all philosophers agree, and the very first step in that direction is the union of husband and wife. Well then, Dante having taken this very wise step, lived an honourable and studious life, being intrusted by his fellow-citizens with many public offices till he attained to the dignity of Prior in 1300, and from this event arose his exile and all the misfortunes of his later life. This is established by an interesting *verbatim* extract from a letter written by

Dante himself. This letter no longer exists, but no doubt Lionardo had seen it, and probably even the autograph itself, for he tells us a few pages further on that he was familiar with Dante's handwriting, which he describes minutely, *secondo io ho veduto in alcune pistole di sua propria mano scritte.* It is well known that all trace of any autograph of Dante has now perished, or at least none whatever is known to exist. This extract is therefore specially valuable and interesting. It is as follows: "All my ills and all my troubles," writes Dante, "had their beginning and origin from my unlucky election as Prior. Though in respect of mature wisdom I was not worthy of this office, yet in loyalty I was not unworthy of it, nor in age, for ten years had elapsed since the battle of Campaldino, in which the Ghibelline party was, so to speak, utterly slain and destroyed, where I found myself no mere child in the practice of arms, and where I was in great fear, and in the end rejoiced greatly through the varying fortunes of that battle."[1] "These," adds Lionardo, "are Dante's own words." It will be observed that the perfectly continuous narrative of Lionardo entirely excludes any possibility of a visit by Dante to Paris in the early

[1] This is explained by the fuller account of the battle already given by Lionardo, who states that the complete rout of the Florentines at the beginning of the fight tempted the Aretines to such a headlong and disorderly pursuit, that from this followed the complete change in the aspect of the battle, and their own total discomfiture in the end.

part of his life. He then proceeds to describe with considerable minuteness the state of factions at Florence and the events and policy of Dante's priorate. He purposes thus to supply a serious defect in Boccaccio's Life, possibly, as he suggests, due to his having had little knowledge[1] on the subject, whereas Lionardo himself, having written a history of Florence, had had occasion to devote special attention to it. Then we have the usual account of the strife of Guelfs and Ghibellines, and the further subdivision of Guelfs into *Bianchi* and *Neri*, originating in Pistoia, and thence imported into Florence. Each of the parties approached the Priors with complaints against the other as disturbers of the public peace, and each in turn demanded their official protection. By the advice of Dante, the Priors, having first quietly taken precautions to strengthen themselves by popular support, took the bold but wise step of banishing the leaders of *both* parties. Dante had no doubt already formed the conviction which he so emphatically pronounced of Guelf and Ghibelline alike many years later,

"Che forte a veder è qual più si falli".[2]

Lionardo then gives the names of the principal leaders on both sides, who were thus impartially banished. However the heads of the Bianchi were soon afterwards allowed to return, and this

[1] Boccaccio, however, in his Commentary, *Lez.* 40 (ii. p. 225), enters pretty fully into this matter.

[2] *Par.* vi. 102.

was one of the chief counts in the accusation
against Dante. His reply was twofold : (1) That
at the time of their return he was no longer in
office. (It will be remembered that this singular
office of Prior was held for two months only,—
in Dante's case from June 15 to August 15,
1300,—"the Florentines having, as Mr. Lowell
observes, made the office bimestral, in order
apparently to secure at least six constitutional
chances of revolution in the year".) (2) There
was a reason for making a distinction, since
Serezzana, the place of their banishment, was so
unhealthy, that Dante's own friend Guido Cavalcanti, in delicate health when banished, soon
sickened and died there. The touching reference to him in the grand episode of Farinata
degli Uberti in *Inf.* x. will be remembered, and
especially the remarkable terms in which Dante
replies to the inquiry of Guido's father, who
suspected, from an ambiguous expression used by
Dante, that his son might be already dead. His
significant reply was, "that his son was still
united with the living,"—

"Che il suo nato è co' vivi ancor congiunto".[1]

His life was then (April 1300), hanging by a
slender thread, very soon indeed to be broken.
Lionardo expressly says that the partiality thus
displayed towards the Bianchi induced Boniface VIII. to redress the balance by sending Charles

[1] Line 111.

of Valois to Florence. He then adds some interesting details, explaining how it was that Charles
not only espoused the cause of the Neri entirely,
but drove out the Bianchi, root and branch, from
Florence. He says that one of his nobles had
been tampered with by three leaders of the
Bianchi (whose names he gives), that he might
induce Charles to take their side, offering to make
him governor of Prato, as the reward for his good
offices. The letter, duly signed and sealed, was
shown to Charles, which so moved his indigna-
tion, that he immediately took the opposite side
without reserve or hesitation. "This letter," says
Lionardo, "I have myself seen, because it is still
preserved in the Florentine archives, but I believe it to be a forgery." Then follow the usual
details of Dante's banishment and condemnation,
related with much minuteness and care, but, as
they are well known, we need not repeat them
here.

Lionardo then proceeds to describe Dante's
life in exile, and this also is done much more
fully than in Boccaccio, especially as regards the
earlier movements both of himself and his companions in exile; how they gathered at Arezzo,
and elected a Council of twelve, of whom Dante
was one, and how, after minor attempts and dis-
appointments, they made a grand final effort in
1304 (it was on July 22), which was very nearly
indeed successful, for they actually captured one
of the gates of Florence. It is not quite certain

whether Dante himself actually took part in this
attack. Some have inferred from *Par.* xvii. 61,
etc., that he did not, but we are simply in the
region of conjecture as to this point, since the
disgust expressed with his associates in the passage referred to may have arisen later, for we
have seen that at any rate at first he co-operated
actively with them. Dante, however, abandoning
all hope of securing his return by force, retired
to Verona, and adopted the language of remon-
strance in several letters addressed to individual
citizens of Florence, and also in one of considerable
length to the people generally, beginning in the
language of Scripture, *Popule mi, quid feci tibi?*
[This again does not appear among his extant
Epistles.] His pleadings however fell on deaf
ears. On the arrival of Henry VII. in Italy, the
exile, once more hopeful, adopted towards the
Florentines a defiant and reproachful tone. Lionardo here probably refers to the Epistle usually
numbered vi., dated March 31, "in the first
year of the most propitious journey of the
Emperor Henry to Italy", and entitled, *Dantes
Allagherius Florentinus et exul immeritus, sceles-
tissimis Florentinis intrinsecus*—"Dante, etc., to
the most rascally Florentines within the city",—
which was certainly not a conciliatory mode of
address. After the death of Henry in 1313,
Dante felt, says Lionardo, that the language he
had lately employed towards those in power at
Florence had finally barred all hopes of his

return. He now acquiesced in the inevitable, and
after wandering about in considerable poverty
from place to place in Lombardy, Tuscany, and
Romagna, he settled at last in Ravenna, and
died there. Observe that Lionardo gives no hint
of a journey to France or England at this time of
his life, any more than at the earlier period. It
is singular that it should have been wholly
omitted, as at one time or another it certainly
appears probable that he visited France at any
rate. Yet the pathetic passage near the beginning
of the *Convito*, in which Dante describes his
wandering life in exile, seems to me to make it
improbable that such a journey had been undertaken at any rate *then*. He there describes himself as " per le parti quasi tutte *alle quali questa
lingua si stende* peregrino". Had he wandered
still further, and into *foreign* lands, he would
scarcely have failed to mention it here as a
further aggravation of his bitter lot.

Lionardo then proceeds to mention some details
of Dante's private life. He states that his means,
though not ample, were sufficient, and he mentions, with apparent precision of knowledge, two or
three distinct places where he possessed property.
His house was richly furnished, according to his
own statement (*secondo egli scrive*).

Lionardo then gives an interesting notice of a
portrait of Dante, then existing " in the Church of
Santa Croce, about the middle of the Church, on
the left-hand side, going towards the high altar.
It was admirably drawn from life (*al naturale*),

by a consummate painter of his own time ". Who,
it may be wondered, was this ? We might naturally suppose Giotto. This is in fact definitely
stated (as we shall see) by Manetti (*inf.* p. 89),
though perhaps, like ourselves, he is only guessing.
Brunone Bianchi states (I know not on what
authority) that this was a fresco by Taddeo
Gaddi (whose date was 1300-1352), and that it
was on a *tramezzo* (*i.e.* a cross-wall or screen, similar, I suppose, to those so common in Spanish
Churches), which was destroyed by Vasari, by
order of Cosimo I., in 1566, when of course its
frescoes also perished. Passing over some interesting personal details, to be referred to later, we
next have a digression of some length upon
Poetry in general (as, it will be remembered, was
the case in Boccaccio's Life), and finally, an estimate of Dante himself, both as a poet and a prose
writer. Lionardo explains that there are two
classes of poets, evidently following out the idea
found in Aristotle, *Poetics*, Chapter XVII. § 2, διὸ
εὐφυοῦς ἡ ποιητική ἐστιν ἢ μανικοῦ κ.τ.λ.[1]   He

---

[1] Lionardo, it may be remarked in passing, was an enthusiastic admirer of Aristotle. He translated the *Ethics*
and other treatises of Aristotle, besides portions of several
other Greek authors. In his Epistles he criticises with extreme severity the existing translations of Aristotle (see
Book iv. last Ep. but one), and justifies the fierceness of
his attack by saying that he feels towards these wretched
translators as he would towards any one whom he found
throwing mud at a picture of Giotto : "Equidem si in pictura
Jotti quis faecem projiceret, pati non possem ; quid ergo
existimas mihi accidere quum Aristotelis libros omni pictura
pretiosiores tanta traductionis faece coinquinari videam " ?

explains that one class of poets arises "da alcun vigore interno e nascoso, il quale si chiama *furore*". (This represents evidently Aristotle's μανικοί. A similar sentiment is also found in Plato.) Lionardo gives a very good illustration of this kind of genius in another field, from the case of S. Francis, *che quasi si trasfigurava oltre al senso umano, e conosceva d' Iddio più che nè per istudio nè per lettere conoscono i Teologi.* The other class of poets he describes as *Poeti litterati e scientifici*, who compose *per istudio, per disciplina ed arte e per prudenza* (evidently again Aristotle's εὐφυεῖς or ἐξεταστικοί). He then adds, *E di questa seconda spezie fu Dante.*[1] He next discourses at length on the Greek derivation of the word "poet" itself, which he says is a matter not generally known to our modern poets, and no wonder, as they are ignorant of Greek. He says that if asked why Dante wrote in the *lingua volgare* rather than in Latin, he would reply at once, because Dante knew that he could do it so much better. In the *volgare* his style is

---

[1] With this estimate of Dante's poetic character Mr. Ruskin agrees, as appears from the following appreciative passage in *Modern Painters*, vol. iii. p. 165 : " Dante has entire command of himself, and can look around calmly, at all moments, for the image or word that will best tell what he sees in the upper or the lower world. . . . It is the highest power in a writer to check all such [*i.e.* artificial] habits of thought, and to keep his eyes fixed on the *pure fact*, out of which if any feeling comes to him or his reader, he knows it must be a true one." In the words of Aristotle, Dante is essentially ἐξεταστικὸς and not μανικός.

eccellentissimo sopra ogni altro, but in Latin verse and in prose (evidently, I think, from the context meaning prose generally, and Italian in particular rather than Latin), he scarcely reaches moderate excellence (*non aggiunse a quelli appena che mezzanamente hanno scritto*), and indeed in the age in which he lived prose writing was not cultivated. Any learning at all to be found in prose writers of that period was limited to the monkish or scholastic style (*al modo fratesco e scolastico*).

Lionardo cites the *Eclogues* of Dante as a proof of the inferiority of his Latin verses to those in the *volgare*; and though he admits that they are good, he maintains that there are plenty better, though no one could say this of his *rima volgare*. It is enough merely to mention the names of his principal predecessors in this art to secure the admission of his pre-eminence over them in every respect. Lionardo adds that it is the opinion of competent judges that no one ever will surpass Dante *in dire in rima*. In fact " before him there arose not any like him, neither after him shall be such". Surely the lapse of five hundred years has not impugned the judgment or falsified the prediction of the biographer. He concludes with a brief notice of his works. He does not add much to our knowledge when he repeats the traditional statement that the *Commedia* was commenced before his banishment, and completed in exile. He does not however

mention the story about the loss of the first seven
cantos.   He praises very highly the *Canzoni*,
but considers the Sonnets to be less successful.
He criticises the *De Monarchia* as *scritto a modo
disadorno senza niuna gentilezza di dire*.   He
dismisses the *De Vulgari Eloquio* (or *Eloquentia*
as he calls it), the *Epistles* and *Eclogues* with a
mere mention, referring briefly also to Dante's
abortive attempt at composing the *Commedia*
in Latin hexameters.   It is most remarkable
that he omits all mention of the *Vita Nuova* and
the *Convito*.   He probably despised the former
as a *leggierezza*, only worthy of notice by such
triflers as Boccaccio ; but it is certainly difficult
to explain his entirely ignoring the *Convito*, to
which no such opinion could attach.

The Life ends with a very pleasing little
personal anecdote.   " Dante," he says, " left a son
Piero, who was a lawyer, and became a very
flourishing man, partly from his own ability, and
partly by the help of his father's name.   He
finally established himself and his family at
Verona.   He had a son called Dante, and this
Dante again had a son called Lionardo, who is
still living, and has several children.   Not long
ago," he proceeds, " this Lionardo visited Florence,
. . . and he came to see me as a friend of the
memory of his great-grandfather Dante.   And I
showed him the homes of Dante and of his
ancestors, and gave him information about many
things to him unknown, since he and his had

been estranged from their native city." And then he concludes his work with a brief reflection evidently suggested by the well-known passage in *Inf.* vii. : *E così la fortuna questo mondo gira, e permuta gli abitatori col volgere di sue rote.*

So ends this interesting contribution to our knowledge of Dante's life. We feel that we have here the work of a serious and intelligent historian, who avoids repeating gossip and, for the most part, also mere current tradition—possibly some might say he does this too rigidly, alarmed by the warning example of Boccaccio ; one too who knows how to make use of letters, archives, and other documents in order to verify or test his statements ; one, finally, who can secure both these merits without becoming dull, since his work is often enlivened by gleams of humour and touches of sympathy.

CHAPTER V.

GIANNOZZO MANETTI lived from 1396 to 1459. He was a scholar, theologian, and diplomatist, and the author of a *Chronicon Pistoriense* and several minor works.

The life of Dante by Manetti is written in Latin, and is fully double the length of that of Lionardo, which was itself nearly half as long again as that of Villani. We can dispose of it however more briefly, only noticing anything distinctive either in the way of addition or omission, as compared with the Lives already analysed. It is one of a series of three lives : Dante, Petrarch, and Boccaccio. The writer's purpose is thus set forth in his preface. Considering, he says, that Boccaccio, Villani, and Lionardo have preceded him, some apology is needed for undertaking the task afresh. But (1) the admiration nowadays felt or expressed for these three consummate poets (*i.e.* Dante, Petrarch, and Boccaccio) is somewhat ignorant and unintelligent. With the learned, at any rate, their reputation rests mainly upon their Latin works. This ought not to be. Manetti therefore desires that on their truest merit, their

Italian writings, and with the most learned and
competent classes of their countrymen, they
should receive the honour they deserve. Were
they living now, or were they conscious of our
praise, it is certain that they would desire
laudari a laudatis viris. (2) Boccaccio wrote
the life of Dante only, Lionardo those of Dante
and Petrarch only ; hence Boccaccio at any rate
still awaits his *vates sacer*, since the work of
Villani, in respect of the Life of Boccaccio, and
indeed of all his Lives, was very poor and meagre :
he wrote *jejune et exiliter*. On these grounds
then Manetti says that he undertook his work,
trusting that he might secure for these three
great Italian poets among the learned that admiration *quae in plebeculâ hactenus latere vide-
batur.*

He begins with the usual account, though at
greater length, of the antecedents of Dante's
family, and the previous fortunes of Florence.
He notices the doubt as to whether Attila or Totila
was its destroyer,[1] and leaves it open, as though
it were a matter incapable of solution. The
Aldigherii (*sic*) [2] are traced (as in Boccaccio, and
as usually) to Ferrara, and not (as in Villani) to
Parma. He correctly states Clement IV. to have
been the reigning Pope at the time of Dante's
birth (it being, as will be remembered, a
common error to write Urban IV.). He mentions

[1] See Supplementary Notes.
[2] The final form of the family name is given as "Aligherus ".

the prophetic dream of Dante's mother, and protests against the scepticism which would deny or doubt it. He regards it as absolutely certain, partly because such visions have frequently happened in the case of great men, notably in those of the tyrant Dionysius and the poet Virgil; partly because the alleged prophecy was verified by the event; and partly also because it is narrated by a grave and well-informed writer (no doubt referring to Boccaccio).

As a boy, Dante displayed extreme aptitude for learning even from the first, and that in spite of the distractions of the most consuming and ardent love—an almost unparalleled circumstance at such an age—for a most beautiful girl, *quamquam cujusdam formosissimae puellae (mirabile dictu) ardentissimis amoribus teneretur.* Manetti, like other biographers, is careful to insist in the strongest terms on the absolute purity of this affection on both sides from first to last.[1] The name Beatrice Portinari is given, as in Boccaccio, and the circumstances of their first meeting are related, including such details as the various occupations and amusements of the guests; and how the little boy Dante, who had been brought there by his parents, was dismissed, when the feast was over, to play with the children, while the elders amused themselves with music and dancing.

---

[1] "Tantus tamen et tam vehemens amorum ardor ita invicem honestus fuit, ut ne minimus quidem aspectus inter se turpis ullo unquam tempore apparuerit."

This is very similar to the corresponding passage in Boccaccio. Dante not long afterwards [1] lost his father, but being placed in the hands of the celebrated Brunetto Latini, made astonishing progress in all branches of knowledge. We then have a passage which is almost a repetition of, and perhaps copied from, Lionardo, as to Dante's sociable life among his fellows, and as to his being present at the great battle of Campaldino; the details of the battle itself, and the part taken in it by Dante, being minutely described, just as in Lionardo.

Then comes the usual account of his grief at the death of Beatrice, which was so vehement that (in the elegant antithesis of the writer) " he ate little and slept even less ". Next, how he took a wife in the year 1291 at the advice of his friends, and here we meet again with the minute and piquant details so gratifying to idle curiosity, so suspicious, and more than suspicious, to sober judgment. This time they are accumulated very much to the injury of the memory of poor Gemma Donati. Boccaccio indeed gave the rein to his very lively imagination on this subject, but was careful to tell us at the end that it was all pure conjecture, and that he had no knowledge that Dante's domestic experience was in fact anything like what he had described. Let us now see how unscrupulously the biographer of nearly a century later lays on his colours. Dante's marriage had not the happy result anticipated by his friends, for, as the writer

[1] " In extrema pueritia mortuo patre."

in his usual bombastic style, and with villanous Latinity, explains—*nimirum omnipotens fortuna sibi adversata videtur.* He found his wife exceedingly morose (*morosam admodum*), just in fact what Socrates found his wife Xanthippe to be. This added to his former distress of mind; for he had to try to put up with his wife's perverse temper at home, lest, if he betrayed his feelings abroad, he should be assailed by the petulant reproaches of the other members of her sex. For a long time he contrived thus to endure the stupid obstinacy of his wife (*stultam uxoris pervicaciam*). But at last, when her intolerable impudence (*intoleranda impudentia*) came to be past all endurance, he left her altogether; but even so, having thus practically effected a divorce, he found things still almost unendurable. Poor Gemma Donati! Was there ever a more heartless and utterly unfounded slander? Yet a good deal that has since been said and written and taken for granted on this subject has no better foundation than this. It is interesting to compare with this baseless gossip the reticence or guarded utterances of earlier and more soberminded biographers; and it is not uninstructive thus to get, as it were, behind the scenes, and to "assist" at the "making of history".

Next we have the usual details at much length of the factions at Florence and the events of Dante's Priorate, including the secret negotiations mentioned by Lionardo (to whom Manetti evidently is largely indebted throughout), between the Whites and Count Ferranti, one of the "Satraps" (as Manetti pompously calls him) of Charles of Anjou, together with the exile and condemnation of Dante and the White faction generally. Then follows a very long and stilted tirade against Florence for her treatment of Dante, freely imitated (including several of the classical allusions and illustrations) from the Seventh Chapter of the *Vita* of Boccaccio. Note that this is a passage occurring in the *Vita* only, and not in the *Compendio*. The usual details as to the early halting-places of Dante's exile follow.[1] It is definitely stated—though we have already learnt to attach very little authority to any assertions made by this writer unless we can "verify his references"—that the love of study took Dante to Paris, where he distinguished himself greatly in theological disputations. He was recalled to Italy by the advent there of Henry VII. The Emperor's movements are minutely described by Manetti, and especially how

---

[1] It should be noted however that Manetti states that it was after some years of exile, and when return appeared hopeless, that Dante betook himself to Verona ; whereas Boccaccio represents him as going there *nel primo fuggire.* Manetti is clearly indebted for his details here to the life of Lionardo, though he boldly states that Dante was kindly received by Alberto Scala at Verona. This error, since Alberto died in 1301, is avoided by Lionardo, and Manetti probably copied the name from Boccaccio, and from the *Vita,* not the *Compendio,* since in the latter the name does not occur. See *sup.* p. 20.

at last he assumed the Imperial Crown in Rome itself, in spite of the opposition chiefly of " Robert, the renowned King of Sicily ",[1] and the people of Florence. After the death of Henry, Dante's sojourn at Ravenna is described with some new and suspicious details, both as to the circumstances of his settlement there,[2] and his occupations when so settled. In particular he is said to have taught many, who afterwards became distinguished men, the Art of Poetry, and the use of their own mother tongue, *ita ut nonnulli ex his vulgares (ut aiunt) non vulgares Poetae haberentur.*[3] After minute details of his personal

---

[1] This was Robert, king of Apulia, third son of Charles II. (*il Ciotto*), who had left him his heir to the throne (1309), disinheriting thereby his grandson Caroberto, son of Carlo Martello. The latter, who had died 1295, was an especial friend of Dante, and the only one among his personal friends whom he honours with a place in Paradise. (See *Par.* VIII.)

[2] *E.g.*, Boccaccio's sober account of the courteous and pressing invitation of Guido is amplified with the most bombastic details. It was conveyed by repeated letters and embassies (*seu per epistolas seu per legatos . . . rogans etiam atque etiam*); it was backed by the most lavish promises, etc. (*quod ut facilius ab eo impetraret, non modo, ut ait Terentianus ille, montes aureos pollicebatur* !). So also Guido himself, whom Boccaccio merely describes as *ne' liberali studi ammaestrato*, now appears as *Vir in omni doctrinarum genere prae ceteris principibus eruditus* !

[3] There is a tradition, repeated in different quarters with more or less distinctness, of Dante's having occupied himself in public teaching at Ravenna. We find it first somewhat vaguely in Boccaccio *Vita*, Chapter VI., *con le sue dimostrazioni fece più scolari in poesia e massimamente nella vulgare.* This reappears with some expansion and more detail (as we

appearance (which I reserve as in other cases),
we meet for the first time with the familiar story
that the old women of Ravenna, seeing Dante
passing in the streets, said one to another, " See
the man who visits hell, and brings back to
the living news of the shades that abide
there". " Yes," replied another, "and his
crisped beard and dark colour, caused by the
gloom and smoke of those regions, evidently
prove your words to be true." Manetti says
that there were two portraits of Dante extant,
both by Giotto, one in the Church of Santa

should expect) in the passage of Manetti quoted in the text.
Saviozzo da Siena (died *c*. 1409) much more definitely still—

> " Qui (*sc.* a Ravenna) cominciò a legger Dante in pria
> Rettorica vulgare, e molti aperti
> Fece di sua poetica armonia ".

(See *Rime di Cino da Pistoia ed altri del Sec.* xiv., by
Carducci, p. 576.)

There is also a curious tradition of his having supported
himself for some time during his exile by keeping a school
at Gubbio. See (*inter alia*) an unedited MS. at Florence,
(cited by Lubin, *Studi*, p. 88) entitled *Teleutologia*, profess-
ing to be written by a pupil who had learned Greek (!) from
Dante. His name is Ubaldo Bastione. Happily for him this
was before the days of examinations ! Dante also addressed
a sonnet (if genuine ?) to Busone da Gubbio—the author
of the well-known Capitolo, *Però che sia*, etc., which
appears in so many MSS. of the *Divina Commedia*—in which
he reports that Busone's son

> " S'avaccia nello stil Greco e Francesco ",

from which it is inferred that he also was one of Dante's
pupils. The sonnet is given by Fraticelli, *Canzoniere*,
p. 282.

Croce[1] (as, it will be remembered, Lionardo stated, though he was not apparently aware of the name of the artist), and the other in the *Capella Praetoris Urbani, i.e.,* I suppose, in the Chapel of the Bargello, and presumably identical with that which was discovered a few years ago, with which every one is now familiar. Then follow numerous details as to Dante's property, and as to his manners and character, obviously copied (and as usual without any acknowledgment) straight from Lionardo, and the story of the book read by him in the apothecary's shop at Siena, in like manner borrowed from Boccaccio. (It occurs, be it observed, in the *Vita,* and not in the *Compendio.*) Further, he tells the story of Dante's marvellous display of memory at Paris,[2] when he dealt with fourteen different abstruse and difficult points of theology *seriatim,* which were hurled at him all at once by several opponents. Manetti says that he could give many other proofs besides this of the same intellectual power, if he chose. We may perhaps take the liberty to doubt this, since this is the only anecdote found in the chapter of Boccaccio's *Vita* from which he is deliberately copying. There is one advantage to be gained from the servile fidelity of his plagiarism, viz. that we gather distinct

[1] See on this what was said *supra,* p. 76.
[2] Py the way he gives an astonishing date for this visit to Paris — *quo se* POST FEDERICI AUGUSTI OBITUM . . . *mox retulerat.*

evidence that he had before him the *Vita* of
Boccaccio, and not the *Compendio,* as any one
will see plainly by referring to the passage.[1] He
next honours the "jejune and meagre" Villani,
by copying the passage at the commencement of
his work about the 900 years-long sleep of Poetry
from which Dante awoke her, showing the
support she might render to Christian Truth,
a passage I have already quoted above (p. 58).
We next have Dante's proud refusal to return to
Florence on humiliating conditions, and (rather
out of place chronologically, but exactly in the
same context as in Boccaccio) his arrogant
saying in reference to the embassy to Boniface,[2]
the story moreover being sadly spoilt in the
telling. A list of his works follows. The *Vita
Nuova* and *Convito* are glibly assigned to his
youth, and the *Commedia* to his advanced years.
The story of its commencement in Latin hexameters is repeated with the additional fact (or
fiction) that he had proceeded very elegantly in
the same style through several cantos before he
changed his purpose. He was occupied over

---

[1] Other indications of this have been noticed, pp. 87 (*bis*),
90, and another occurs in the next note.

[2] Manetti, being apparently a little uncertain about his
French history, here cautiously describes Charles of Valois
as *Carolum quendam vel Philippi Francorum Regis fratrem
vel potius propinquum,* showing plainly that he is copying
the *Vita* of Boccaccio—*un fratello ovvero congiunto di Filippo
allora re di Francia* (*c.* xii.). These words do not occur in
the *Compendio.*

this about twenty-five years[1] or more, *since*—(note again the interesting process by which history is manufactured)—" since before his exile he had completed seven cantos, which the Greeks[2] call *Odes*". As Manetti tells us that Dante was 56 when he died, and 35 in 1300, and consequently 36 when exiled, you subtract 36 from 56, remainder 20, and throw in about 5 years for planning out the work, and completing seven cantos of it,[3] as he would no doubt not get on so fast before his exile as afterwards, when he was less interrupted by public duties. Indeed, Manetti with the utmost *naïveté* goes on to explain that in this manner *luce clarius apparet* that this must have been just the time occupied by the *Commedia*. A short notice is added of the *Epistles, Eclogues* and *De Monarchia*. The *De Vulgari Eloquio* is not mentioned. The story of the Venetian Embassy resulting in his death from fever contracted in the land journey homewards, combined with vexation of mind at the treatment which he had received at Venice, is then told, as in Villani. Then the Life concludes with the account of his funeral, and the epitaphs on his tomb. He says that *ab initio* the epitaph

[1] It should be noticed that Villani in two passages assigns about twenty-three years to the composition of the *Divina Commedia*.

[2] So also (which is perhaps more to the point) does Villani (*sup.* p. 61).

[3] "Nam aliquot annos in septem illarum odarum absolutione consumsisse credendum est."

Theologus Dantes, etc., was carved there. Afterwards the six lines *Jura Monarchie,* etc., being
far more elegant than the others, and the composition of some very learned man (*a doctissimo
quodam viro edita*) replaced the former, which
were erased. I have spoken of the difficulties
involved in these statements in the article on
the Tomb of Dante, already more than once
referred to.

In conclusion, we feel that this prolix and
rather pretentious work has added little either to
our knowledge or to our pleasure. Its only feature
of originality is displayed in the inventive
enterprise of the author, while the rest is a
mere *réchauffé* of Boccaccio and Lionardo, with
occasional scraps from Villani. The net result may
be given in the well-known language of Sydney
Smith—" There is much that is new in this work,
and also much that is true ; but unfortunately
that which is new is not true, and that which is
true is not new."

CHAPTER VI.

THE LIFE BY FILELFO.

GIOVANNI MARIO FILELFO (1426-1480) was the son of the much more distinguished Francesco Filelfo, who lived 1398-1481, thus surviving his son by one year. Giovanni Mario led an erratic and eccentric life, and though by profession an advocate, was better known as a *littérateur*. He was a somewhat prolific poet, and, as we shall see, did not limit the play of his fancy to his poetical works.

The Life of Dante by Filelfo (which is in Latin), though written soon after the middle of the fifteenth century, was never published till 1828,[1] and, as it has not been republished, it is now very rare and difficult to meet with. It was hardly to be expected that at that date (*c*. 1450) many new facts respecting the life of the poet could be produced, except perhaps by a diligent search into archives and official documents. But as the date was too late for authentic personal reminiscences, so it was too early for the careful and critical research

---

[1] *Vita Dantis Aligherii a J. Mario Philelpho scripta.* Florence : 1828.

which is the peculiar merit of more modern works.
The authority on which Filelfo mainly depends,
and it seldom or never fails him, is his own most
airy and lively imagination, unembarrassed by any
references to documents, except when he is
servilely copying the very language of Lionardo,
or Boccaccio, or others of his predecessors. A
brief analysis, with extracts of some of the most
striking points, will enable my readers to judge
of this for themselves.

He makes a good start by saying that Cacciaguida had a son called Aliger, *eo dictus quod ea
familia gereret Alam in signo.*[1] This in any
case would be a curious "putting of the cart
before the horse", but as a matter of fact the
arms referred to were not the original arms of the
family—these may be found in Pelli, Lord Ver-
non's work, and elsewhere—the canting heraldry
of the wing (*or*) on a field (*azure*) having been
adopted much later, and apparently after the
settlement of the family in Verona. There is
said to be distinct evidence that even in Dante's
time (viz. 1302), the old arms were still used.[2]
Filelfo provides for Dante a very complete
education, not only in all branches of literature,
but also in the management of horses, and sport-
ing dogs (*canes ad venandum*), and the use of the
bow, the *scorpio*, the spear, and the sword, and

---

[1] Benvenuto hazards a more surprising suggestion as follows :—*Quasi* ALTA DIGERENS *vel* ALIA DIGERENS *quam alii
poetae* (!), p. 12.   [2] Editor's note, *h.l.*

in every kind of military exercise.[1] We then have a long digression on the importance of literature, because, as we are surprised to learn, *doctrina Lacedaemonios nobilitavit, Athenienses stabilivit, Romanis imperium orbis tradidit.* It has not been usual to attribute the power of either Sparta or Rome to the successful cultivation of literature.

Then at the battle of Campaldino, Dante's exploits were such *ut vix aut dici posset aut excogitari.* Filelfo is not satisfied with borrowing from Lionardo the statement that Dante described the battle in an Epistle, but adds *declaratque se iisce interfuisse ac praefuisse rebus* (p. 17). He then further copies from Lionardo (without acknowledgment, of course) the expression of regret that Boccaccio did not devote his attention to these exploits, instead of the childish nine-year-old love. Filelfo then strikes out a very bold line, anticipating the brilliant scepticism of modern critics, by stating that in his opinion Beatrice was a pure myth—there never was such a person at all,—she was just as real as Pandora.[2]

---

[1] *Equos alere aut canes ad venandum, aut arcu scorpioneve ac ense et hasta uti ad omnem militarem meditationem* (p. 11). The *scorpio* is explained by Isidore to be *sagitta venenata arcu vel tormentis excussa.* It is mentioned by Pliny, *Nat. Hist.* vii. 56, among a list of various national missiles—*venabula et in tormentis scorpionem Cretas invenisse dicunt.*

[2] "Ego aeque Beatricem quam amasse fingitur Dantes mulierem unquam fuisse opinor ac fuit Pandora."

Moreover that Dante's childish love itself was a pure invention, and *fictam . . . esse rem omnem*! And as to Dante's addressing poems to her being any proof, have not poets often also invented dreams, naval battles, and military engines, which never had any existence out of the poet's brain? But Boccaccio, being Cupid's slave and the Prince of Lovers, took his standard of the love of Virtue and the delight of Happiness. from sensual Pleasure.[1] "Being earthly, he speaks of the earth." *Tractant fabrilia fabri,* he adds (which in this context might be roughly paraphrased, "Boccaccio cannot help *talking shop*"). This, it will be remembered, is extremely unfair to Boccaccio, as he is most careful to insist with the utmost emphasis on the absolute purity of Dante's affection, and its entire freedom from any such associations as these. After Campaldino Dante returned to Florence, and was a model of gravity, propriety, and learning, always among the doctors (*in doctorum corona*), "hearing them or asking them questions." *A propos* of this, we have a *réchauffé* of Lionardo's protest against unsociable students (see *supra*, p. 69). Dante married as a young man, though Filelfo omits all mention of his being urged to it by the solicitation of his friends. He probably thought this quite superfluous, since he says that his wife had very great

---

[1] " Ipse Cupidinis servus . . . Boccaccius amantium princeps amorem virtutis ac beatitudinis jucunditatem secundum carnis voluptates judicavit."

G

wealth, extreme beauty, and this combined with
the utmost modesty, and was also of a most noble
family, a *gem* in character and in form, as well as
in name.[1]   She had in fact all the four qualifications which in the *Tyrant* of Xenophon (*apud
Xenophontis tyrannum*) are to be sought for by
young men looking out for a wife.   After this we
are not surprised to miss any allusions to Dante's
alleged domestic infelicity.   On the contrary, this
ideal description of Gemma—probably quite as
imaginary as the unfavourable suggestions of
Boccaccio, and the deeply blackened portraiture of
Manetti—forms the occasion of a grand outbreak
against Boccaccio for saying that wives generally
are a hindrance to study.   How can this be,
argues Filelfo, with fine logic, if marriage is
natural to man, and society itself is founded upon
marriage?   Then follows a long digression on the
advantages of matrimony (something like the introduction to our marriage service), seasoned with
classical allusions and illustrations, which, by the
way, he steals shamelessly from Lionardo, giving
the same instances, and in the same order (omitting only Cato), viz.: Socrates, Aristotle, Cicero,
Seneca, and Varro.   If young men marry, Filelfo
solemnly proceeds, they settle down steadily, they
spend their nights at home, they give up drinking,
extravagance, and bad company, they save their
money, and endeavour to set a good example to

[1] "Cui nomen erat Gemma, vere (inquam) et moribus et
specie Gemma,"

their sons. Surely all this must be beneficial, not a hindrance, to study. Thus Boccaccio was all wrong from beginning to end. But Dante was aware of all this, and in consequence resolved upon marrying Gemma.

Next we have a description of his public offices, whence, according to his own account, arose all his troubles. Then follows a reference to Dante's own letter, copied straight from Lionardo, as also is the long account of Florentine factions, including the censure of Boccaccio for being so brief on this point. He says that Dante was falsely charged with sending the exiled Whites to Serezzana, *quod commodior esset reditus*, which would imply that he paved the way, *while still in office*, for their early return, though their actual recall took place when he was no longer in authority.[1] The story is given of the *vel vera vel simulata Alborum fraus*—which Lionardo, it will be remembered, pronounced to be *simulata* [2]—in respect of tampering with the officer of Charles of Valois, though, by the way, Filelfo wrongly gives his name as *Ferdinandus* instead of *Ferrantius*. Filelfo explains that Charles was most indignant that he should have been supposed by any one to be capable of being thus tampered with, *qui aequissimus foret et Summi Pontificis nomine missus esset*. The latter consideration would, I fear, afford a very poor guarantee for any one's character in that age. The usual details as to

---

[1] See *sup.* p. 73.   [2] P. 74.

Dante's exile and wanderings follow, burdened with a heavy list of historical parallels of great men exiled in classical times.

The triumphant progress of the Emperor Henry is described, but such was Dante's affection for his native city, that, according to Filelfo, he shrunk from contemplating her impending and, as he thought, inevitable overthrow. This seems hardly consistent with the tone and language of his *Epistles* written at this time (see especially those numbered 5, 6, and 7, *Ed.* Fraticelli).

We then have a wearisome digression, many pages long, full of classical quotations, and of examples of great men who have defied Fortune even as Dante did. The author seems to be pouring out upon us the contents of his common-place book *s.v. Fortuna.* Then, in order to enhance the greatness of Dante's victory over the fickle goddess, he gives the rein to his fancy in truly magnificent style, as to the gifts which Fortune lavished upon Dante in early life. Before his exile she had given him considerable, though not excessive wealth, noble lineage, a brother, a wife, children. His house at Florence was magnificently furnished, much more so, indeed, than was suitable to a private citizen,[1] and

---

[1] We may suppose this to be pure invention, or perhaps a highly coloured expansion of the language of Lionardo, that Dante had *suppellettile abbondante e prezioso, secondo egli scrive.* Lionardo seems to be quoting from one of those numerous letters of Dante to which he refers elsewhere as well known to him.

very much beyond his own means.[1] His furniture and surroundings were worthy of Lucullus (*Lucullina supellex*), and more suitable for Marcus Crassus than Dante Alighieri! His farms, of which he had several, were most productive in corn and wine. His friends were all good and learned men, his clients and dependants without number.[2] Rightly was he called *Dante*, in foresight of his future bounty in a variety of ways, and especially because he *gave* to all men instruction in the right way of life.[3] *Par.* xxvi. 104 is quoted (of course, with the reading *Dante*) to show how fitting it was that Adam, who gave names to all living things, should, as it were, thus ratify that name. He harps on this subject for three or four pages. Also Dante had four sons, as to whose history Filelfo's information seems very inaccurate. To begin with, the names of six are ordinarily recorded: viz. Gabriello and Bernardo, in addition to the four mentioned by Filelfo, who are Pietro, Jacopo, Alighieri, and Eliseo.[4] The last two died, according to Filelfo, of the plague, aged twelve and eight. This *may* be true, but no other trace has been found of any plague at Florence about that time.[5]

---

[1] Filelfo makes Dante himself responsible for this statement by vaguely adding *ut hujus utar de se testimonio.*

[2] "Clientelas habuit infinitas hic poeta."

[3] "Habito suae futurae largitionis multis modis praesagio . . . cunctis hominibus dedit bene vivendi rationem."

[4] See Supplementary Notes.

[5] So says Pelli, *Memorie*, etc., p. 45.

Filelfo says that Jacopo died of Roman fever, when accompanying his father on the Embassy to Boniface in 1301. This is certainly wrong, as there is distinct documentary evidence that he survived his father, and was still living in 1342.[1] Pietro studied at Florence, Siena, and Bologna, and was his father's constant companion in exile, after whose death he settled at Verona, where he became a very wealthy man. He had a son called Jacopo, who wrote a Commentary in verse on his grandfather's poem,[2] in which, according to Filelfo, he made use of his own father Pietro's Commentary, a work which is quite indispensable to all who would expound the *Divina Commedia.* We have the family of Pietro further traced out till we arrive at persons still living.

Passing on from the manifold gifts of Fortune to Dante, Filelfo says he will next give us an account of his personal appearance and character. As before, I reserve these for future notice, only remarking that the usual and familiar details are seasoned and supplemented in a most astonishing manner with unlikely and incongruous, but evidently (in the opinion of Filelfo) desirable

---

[1] See again Pelli, p. 42.

[2] *Rhythmis interpretatus est avi codicem.* This, of course, refers to the so-called *Capitolo* or epitome of Jacopo, beginning *O voi che siete,* and consisting of 154 lines, which is found in so many MSS. of the *Divina Commedia.* But this, as well as the prose Commentary attributed to Jacopo, is always assigned to Dante's *son* Jacopo, whom Filelfo has killed off in 1301.

qualities. During his exile Dante is said to have taken advantage of his enforced leisure to study philosophy at Cremona, logic at Naples, and dialectic at Paris, to the great admiration of the French, who, much as they hate Italians, could not help admiring Dante. Then he went to Can Grande, and at his request wrote an "interpretation" of the *Paradiso*, and dedicated also that work to him. Filelfo adds, *Illos Commentarios integros habeo, et illis delector maximopere.* I suppose he must be referring to the so-called Dedicatory Epistle to Can Grande (No. xi.), and its exposition of the commencement of the *Paradiso*, but this does not extend beyond the first twenty lines. Lionardo is again laid under contribution for a criticism of the Latin Prose style of Dante and other writers of his age. We have the customary remarks about the Greek derivation of the word Poetry, and its relation to Theology (for which *vide* Boccaccio), and about Plato's censure of poets, and also S. Jerome on the same subject (several pages of this). Then follows the regular story of Dante's commencing the *Commedia* in Latin hexameters, and the *usual two-and-a-half lines* are given as a specimen, though Filelfo adds, *processeratque hoc pacto aliquanto diffusius quam voluisset.* Compare Manetti much to the same effect.[1] It is amusing to see how all these writers invariably stop short at the middle of the third line, *Pro meritis cuicunque*

---

[1] See *sup.* p. 91.

suis, adding "etc.", but never giving us a single specimen of a line beyond this, out of all that Dante is supposed to have written afterwards. When it came to definite information, they simply copied one another like sheep—

"E ciò che fa la prima, e l'altre fanno".[1]

A panegyric follows on the variety of Dante's acquirements, viz. rhetoric, geometry, arithmetic, music, astronomy, theology. In the case of astronomy, Filelfo is imprudent enough to give the reason for his assertion. He was an astronomer, he says, of no ordinary kind, "for he foretold many of the calamities of Florence, the wars of Italy, and other political changes, all of which would have been impossible without an accurate knowledge of the movements of the celestial bodies"! His greatest work was styled by himself "a Comedy". Filelfo says that he should have preferred to call it a "Tragi-Comedy", but he adds that he is absolutely debarred from doing so by the *dictum* of Aristotle, *quia fine dicat res omnes denominandas esse.*[2] So we must call it a Comedy after all, as Dante himself did, because it ends happily!

This work, says Filelfo, Dante began at the age of twenty-one, and published it (*edidit*) at the age of forty-two. I am surprised, he says, at those who say that it was begun at thirty-five, on account of the expression *mezzo cammino di nostra vita*

---

[1] *Purg.* iii. 82.

[2] *Nic. Ethics*, iii. 7 : ὁρίζεται ἕκαστον τῷ τέλει.

in *Inferno* i. 1, *i.e. dimidium vitae*, "the half of life". The true explanation of this is to be found in the statement of Aristotle, that in the half of life (*dimidio vitae*) the wise man does not differ from the fool, meaning by *the half of life, sleep.* Hence, Dante meant to say that he was asleep when this experience befell him, or, in other words, that his life was just like that of ordinary men, no better than "a waking dream". *Non est igitur de annis haec descriptio*" (p. 106).[1] Among other works of Dante there was a history in Italian prose of the Guelfs and Ghibellines, of which Filelfo professes to give the opening sentence, adding, "such are his words which he thus committed to the immortality of writing". It would seem to be almost the only case in which he missed the reward of immortality, unless, indeed, we suppose Filelfo to be again drawing on his imagination for his facts. At any rate, no one else mentions such a work, nor has any one been able to find any other trace of it. A brief notice is added of the *De Monarchia* and *De Vulgari Eloquio*, but the *Convito* is not mentioned at all.[2] Finally, he wrote or pub-

[1] Strange to say, this nonsense has not even the questionable merit of originality. It is noticed (generally to reject it), as a possible explanation, by some of the old commentators (e.g. *Pet. Ott. Benv.*). To have excogitated it implies some ingenuity, however perverted. To tamely copy it is the merest ineptitude.

[2] It will be remembered that it was passed over by Lionardo, which may probably account for its omission here.

lished Epistles without number (*edidit et Epistolas innumerabiles*). Of these he mentions three, none of which, I believe, appear among those now extant. (1) One beginning *Magna de te fama*, and addressed to "the invincible king of the Huns". This sounds strange. (2) Another beginning *Beatitudinis tuae sanctitas*, addressed to Boniface VIII.; and (3), a third commencing *Scientia, mi fili*, addressed to his son (Peter, of course) at Bologna. Filelfo adds that there were many others still extant (*quas habent multi*), but which it would be difficult for him to enumerate. That we can well believe.

In reference to the fourteen embassies which Dante is traditionally, but most improbably, said to have been intrusted with, Filelfo states that " he spoke and wrote French well (*non insipide*, p. 117); so at least it is said, but I relate those things only which I know for certain, and which I have myself seen. Anything else I should not venture to assert "!

My readers will probably agree with me that in spite of this very proper, but at the same time very surprising, statement, no further remark is necessary in taking leave of this curious production than that of the Marchese Trivulzio [1]: "To quote Filelfo as an authority for any statement would be no less ridiculous than to appeal to Don Quixote in confirmation of an historical fact".

[1] Quoted by Scartazzini, *Vita di Dante* (Hoepli's Series) p. 8.

The difficulty of procuring or even getting a sight of the work (there is not a single copy in Oxford, even in the Bodleian), must be my apology for having expounded it at greater length than its intrinsic value might seem to deserve.

CHAPTER VII.

OTHER EARLY BIOGRAPHICAL NOTICES.

WE have now gone through the five principal
early biographers of Dante. There are several
other minor works which we might rather perhaps
describe as biographical notices than biographies,
on which a few words may be added.

We notice first the most important of them, and
indeed the earliest record of all, antedating even the
Life by Boccaccio, viz. the well-known chapter
which Giovanni Villani (IX. 136) devotes to this
subject. It is very brief, and the following points
only need be noticed here. The embassy to Venice
is mentioned as having immediately preceded
Dante's death, though there is no hint of the
latter being not only *post hoc*, but *propter hoc*,
as in F. Villani's Life. The very singular
blunder is made that Dante died in July, whereas of course it was on September 14th. He is
there said to have been buried, not only with
great honour, but also in *abito di poeta e gran
filosofo*.[1] He was of an honourable and ancient
Florentine family living near St. Peter's Gate

---

[1] An anonymous *terza rima* poem *laudante el famosissimo
poeta Dante Alighieri di Firenze* in a Bodleian MS. (*Canon.*

(*porta San Piero*), and *a neighbour of ours.*
(Giovanni Villani died 1348, his age, I believe,
not recorded, but as he was intrusted with
a negotiation with Pisa in 1317, he was doubtless old enough to have been familiar with his
illustrious neighbour).[1] *After* his "undeserved
banishment"—(note this date)—Dante went to
study, according to Villani, at Bologna and Paris,
and other parts of the world. His principal
works are there enumerated: the *Vita Nuova*
being the work of his youth; then, during his
exile, twenty *Canzoni*, and three noble Epistles.
These three are those to the citizens of Florence,
to the Emperor Henry VII., and to the conclave of
Cardinals after the death of Clement V. Next
comes the *Commedia*, and then the *De Monarchia*
is briefly mentioned. Then, in a passage which is
wanting in some MSS., the *Convito* is described,
though not mentioned by name, and the *De
Vulgari Eloquentia* (*sic*), of which only two books
out of four were finished. Finally, Villani adds
that though Dante was scornful and contemptuous in his manner, and too apt to wrap himself
up in his superiority as a philosopher, yet his
other virtues, his learning and his patriotism,
make him worthy of obtaining a lasting memo-

Ital. 50, fol. 48, etc.), describes his burial as magnificent, and
adds :—

> "Come vero poeta fu vestito,
> Con la corona in testa dell' alloro,
> In sul pecto un libro ben fornito," etc.

[1] See further Supplementary Notes.

rial by means of this chronicle of ours, though
his noble writings are themselves a true testimony
to his fame.

Several of the early Commentaries on the
Divina Commedia are prefaced by a biographical
notice, as, for instance, those of Benvenuto da
Imola, Landino, Vellutello, and Daniello da
Lucca. The *Ottimo Comento*, though not giving
any formal biography, contains two very interesting notices of the poet's life and habits. In
the note on *Inferno* x. 85, he says that he, the
writer, heard Dante say that he had never been
led for the sake of a rhyme to say anything that
was not otherwise in his mind; but that many
times and oft he had made words signify something other than that which they had been wont
to express in other poets. Again, in the note on
Inferno xiii. 144, the writer says that he got
Dante to narrate to him the traditional account
which he had received and adopted as to the
foundation of Florence and its connection with
Mars. The most interesting, however, of these
minor biographical notices occurs in the unedited
Commentary of Serravalle, since he (and he alone)
is responsible for the statement that Dante visited
Oxford. Of this interesting Commentary only
two MSS. are known to exist. One is in the
Vatican Library (see Colomb de Batines, ii. p. 335),
and the other was happily secured for the British
Museum at the Wodhull sale in 1886. The
Commentary was written by Giovanni Bertoldi,

better known as Giovanni da Serravalle, and it is
stated in the colophon to have been undertaken
at the instance of Cardinal Amidei of Saluzzo;
Nicolas Bubwith, Bishop of Bath and Wells;
and Robert Hallam, Bishop of Salisbury; and to
have been completed on Jan. 16, 1417, while the
author and his patrons were in attendance at the
Council of Constance.[1]   Its chief interest for our
present purpose consists in the eight *Praeam-*
bula prefixed to the Commentary, occupying fif-
teen or sixteen pages in the MS.; and in the fifth
and eighth of these *Praeambula* in particular.
The fifth is headed *Quam Dante se facit dis-*
cipulum Virgilii, etc.   His first meeting with
Beatrice is described, and the writer then romances
in the following astonishing manner:—

"*Subito fuit philocaptus de ipsa, et ipsa de*
ipso (!); *qui se invicem dilexerunt quousque vixit*
ipsa puella (!); *quæ mortua fuit* MCCXC. *Amor*
corum fuit valde honestus.   Post cujus mortem
Dantes tardavit per decem annos antequam inci-
peret hoc opus et hunc librum.   Beatricis tamen
mortue semper remansit ymago gratissima in
mente ipsius Dantis recentis [sic], *non adeo tamen*
quando adhuc Dantes fuerit iterum de novo philo-
captus in Lucca de una alia puella nomine Par-
golecta (!).   *Modo nota quod Dantes dilexit hanc*
puellam Beatricem ystorice et literaliter; sed allego-
rice et anagogice dilexit theologiam sacram, in qua
diu studuit TAM IN OXONIIS IN REGNO ANGLIE,

---

[1] See *supra* under Lionardo, p. 65.

*quam Parisius in regno Francie. Et fuit bacha-
larius in Universitate Parisiensi in qua legit
sententias pro forma magisterii; legit bibliam;
respondidit* [sic] *cuilibet, doctoribus ut mos est; et
fecit omnes actus qui fieri debent per doctorandum
in S. Theologia. Nihil restabat fieri nisi inceptio
seu conventus: et ad incipiendum seu ad faciendum
conventum,* DEERAT SIBI PECUNIA; *pro qua acqui-
renda rediit Florentiam,"* etc. It is then explained
how he was made Prior at Florence, *et neglexit
studium nec rediit Parisius.* In the 8th *Prae-
ambulum* it is again stated that Dante studied
at Padua and Bologna, *demum Oxoniis et Parisius,
ubi fecit multos actus mirabiles.*

Now, much as one would wish to believe that
Dante had visited Oxford, one cannot but remark
that (1) the statement that he did so is first made
in a work written a hundred years after his death,
and is apparently wholly unconfirmed by any
other testimony; (2) it is suspicious that it is
found in a work written to please two English
patrons, one of whom had been Chancellor of the
University of Oxford;[1] (3) the passage in which
the statement occurs contains some palpably
false and purely fabulous statements; (4) it is
worth observing that the sojourn at Paris as well
as Oxford is here said to have taken place in
Dante's youth, and in connection with his education, whereas the visit to Paris, at any rate, is
stated by Boccaccio to have been in consequence

---

[1] Robert Hallam filled this office from 1403 to 1406.

of Dante's exile. The other early biographers
(whether their authority is independent of
Boccaccio or not) either do the same, or exclude
by implication an earlier visit.[1] It should also be
added that a *poetical* passage is sometimes quoted
from Boccaccio which is thought to confirm the
Oxford visit, where among the places visited by
Dante he mentions

" Parisios demum *extremosque Britannos* ".[2]

But we must set against this the significant
silence of the *prose* Life of Boccaccio, where, however, Paris is expressly mentioned.

Another writer of some interest on the subject
is Ser Dino Forestani, more commonly known as
Saviozzo da Siena. He committed suicide in
prison, but was living (from the internal evidence
of one of his poems) at any rate as late as 1409.[3]

---

[1] See *sup.* pp. 60, 72, 76, 87, 103.

[2] This line comes from a Latin Epistle of Boccaccio to
Petrarch, said to have been accompanied by the present of
a copy in Boccaccio's own hand of the *Divina Commedia*—
in fact, the celebrated Vatican ms. (No. 3199), in which
these lines are found. (See Supplementary Notes.)

[3] See for further details Mortara's Catalogue of the Canon-
ici mss. at the Bodleian, pp. 59, 99, etc. The mss. *Canon.
Ital.* 50 and 81 contain several *Canzoni* by Saviozzo from
which I have made the following extracts. There are three
of special interest, written in prison. The first two breathe
a most devout and contrite spirit (each stanza of the first
beginning with the refrain *Domine ne in furore tuo arguas
me*), and are very touching in their tone of abject misery.
They are in strange contrast with No. 3, which is headed
Canzone facta in carcere, la quale è desperata e diabolica.

Among various statements about Dante of an ordinary character, there are only two calling for special remark here. The first concerns the visit to Paris.

"Dopo gli studi Italici, a Parigi[1]
　　Volse abbracciar filosofia e Dio :
　　　Non molto stette poi riveder quici
　　La Scala, i Malespini, il Casentino," etc.

It is to be observed (1) that there is no allusion to England or Oxford in connection with the studies at Paris; (2) that the visit to Paris is stated to have occurred (as the context a few lines earlier shows) during Dante's exile.

The other passage repeats the statement that Dante gave readings in *Rettorica Volgare* at

In his despair he invokes the Furies, Erichthon, Cerberus, Antæus, etc., and after cursing his parents and his birth (like Job), he anticipates with horrible detail, and evident reminiscences of Dante's *Inferno*, the various tortures and monsters with which he will soon be familiar, ending, *Però che Dio m'è contra e'l mondo in ira.* There is another Canzone in MS. No. 81 of the same character, in which he curses at large, viz. the planets, stars, poetry, science, his parents, teachers, etc. etc., adding *e Satanas risurga furibondo*, etc.

[1] We may compare with this the reference in the anonymous *terza rima* Canzone already referred to, *sup.* p. 108 (*note*), where it is said that *after* his banishment *Dante allo studio n' andò a Bologna*, and afterwards, *N' andò ad Parisi, ove d' ogni scientia Fino maestro fu senza menzogna*, etc. It may be added that several expressions in this anonymous *Canzone*, such as " *per quel ch' io sento* ", " *che non ai inteso* ", etc., seem to imply a writer within a generation or so of the events described.

Ravenna. This has been already quoted *supra* under Manetti (p. 88, note 3).

We will conclude this chapter with an account of a very singular and little-known legend, recorded by Matteo Palmieri, a somewhat younger contemporary of Lionardo Aretino, his date being 1405-1475, which is reprinted by Papanti[1] (p. 98), but which I have not seen elsewhere referred to. It is, as will be seen, a pure and simple myth, having no pretension to any connection with history, though apparently recorded as such by the chronicler, since he says that, though he cannot explain or account for the details, the *fact* " m'è per fama certissimo ". The story is told in reference to the battle of Campaldino, in which, as we have already seen, Dante took part, and is evidently constructed from a reminiscence of the myth at the end of Plato's *Republic*, respecting Er the son of Armenius, with further details suggested by a familiarity with the *Divina Commedia* itself. The pursuit of the enemy and the occupation of Bibbiena and other strongholds having occupied two days, on the third day the victors returned to the scene of the battle, Dante among them, in order to search for their friends and bury the dead. Dante was horror-struck to see the body of a dear friend slain in the battle, though now " τριταῖος γενόμενος ", start up and address him.[2]

---

[1] *Dante secondo la Tradizione e i Novellatori.* Livorno. 1873.

[2] The chronicler cautiously adds—*o risuscitato o non morto che fusse, m' è incerto.*

He informs Dante that by special favour he has
been allowed to return to life for a short time to
tell him what he has seen *infra le due vite in
questi tre dì.* As soon as Dante has recovered
from his fright he proceeds to cross-question his
friend as to certain practical difficulties in the
modus operandi of this strange occurrence. His
friend tells him that he is not able to satisfy
such inquiries; Dante must in fact be *contento
. . . al quia* (*Purg.* iii. 37), and listen to the important revelation he has to make. He then proceeds to relate, with sundry obvious reminiscences
of phrases and details out of the *Divina Commedia,*
what his experience has been. "Whether in
the body or out of the body" he cannot tell,
he was confronted by an intensely brilliant orb
of light (afterwards explained to be the moon).[1]
He was soon accosted by an old man *di
reverente autorità.* [Compare the beginning of
the *Purg.* when the four stars shed a light as
though the sun were before him (l. 39), and the
vision of Cato as *un veglio . . . Degno di tanta
riverenza in vista,* etc.] The old man in this case,
of all strange guides in such surroundings, turns
out to be Charlemagne ! After receiving a panegyric on his noble life and deeds on earth, con-
ceived in the spirit of Dante's address to Virgil,
or Virgil's to Cato, but much more prolix, Charlemagne proceeds to explain the nature of the

[1] "la minima delle sante luci, più che niuna altra dilungi
dal cielo, e vicina alla terra."

heavenly bodies and their influence on the
generation of animals and men, which recalls
the account given in *Par.* vii., to say nothing
of several Dantesque phrases embedded in his
discourse, such as *della sua legge ribello . . . nè
vuole che per lui in sua città si ritorni* (cf. *Inf.* i.
125, 126). So also in the brief description of the
Inferno which follows, we have not only the
usual rivers and other geographical features, and
the principal mythical personages, such as
Cerberus, Pluto, Charon, Minos, etc. (which no
doubt are common property and not peculiar to
Dante), but also such phrases as *per forza di poppa*
(*Inf.* vii. 27) ; *L'anima . . . in questo inferno . . .
ruina* (comp. *Inf.* xxxiii. 133, *Ella ruina in sì
fatta cisterna*). Compare again the phrase *il
centro al quale ricascono tutte le circumstanti gra-
vezze* with *Inf.* xxxiv. 111, *Al qual si traggon
d' ogni parte i pesi,* etc. etc. So again, when entering the heavenly spheres, the contemptible small-
ness of the earth fills the newly arrived wanderer
with amazement, just as Dante notes in two or
three places in the *Paradiso* (*e.g.* xxii. 151, etc.).
The *moral* of the myth, which is again and again
repeated and emphasised, is that God's most
special favour awaits those who have ruled well
(like Charlemagne), or have served their country
in civil or military offices. Hence among the inhabitants of Paradise (which is therefore more
widely thrown open than by Dante), those who
are specially singled out for notice are Fabricius,

Curtius, Fabius, Scipio, and Metellus. So again those who die fighting for their country or devote their lives to promoting unity, and healing discords among their fellow-citizens. For this reason alone the special favour here described is said to have been granted to Dante's friend who narrates his wonderful experiences. The narrative concludes with a final repetition of this moral by Charlemagne. Dante's attempt at a reply is cut short immediately by the sudden fall of the body of his friend, which Dante vainly endeavoured to resuscitate. He therefore proceeded to bury it, and then rejoined the army.

CHAPTER VIII.

PERSONAL TRAITS AND CHARACTERISTICS OF DANTE
AS GATHERED FROM THE EARLY BIOGRAPHERS,
AND ILLUSTRATED BY PASSAGES IN HIS OWN
WRITINGS.

WE proceed now in this concluding chapter to
gather together the personal traits and characteristics of the great poet, as depicted in these early
biographies, illustrating or checking them when
we can from allusions to be found in his own
writings. I will first say a few words on a feature
which is common to all these early biographies,
and one which to some degree, and possibly to
an exaggerated degree, tends in this critical and
matter-of-fact and unimaginative age to detract
from their credit : I mean the more or less anecdotal, not to say gossiping, character which belongs
to them. Notwithstanding this, as I maintained
at the outset, such works have a special interest
and value of their own, and are not superseded
in that respect by the more serious labours of
the chronicler, the historian, or the critic. Still,
nowadays, there is a good deal of very uncom-
fortable scepticism about this lighter department

(if I may so call it) of biography. The first
impulse on reading an interesting anecdote,
or an incident of what we might call modern
character or human interest, which is stated as
having occurred four or five centuries ago, is to
doubt whether it is true. Things of this kind
did happen, I suppose, to people even in the
thirteenth century. Life must then, as now, have
been full of those incidents which make up
anecdotes. If they happened, why should they
not be recorded? If they are recorded, that is
really not in itself a reason why they should be un-
true. And if they *were* true, what other evidence
could be expected than such traditions?—for
assuredly they could not be looked for in state
archives. A witty friend of mine once said that
the reason why it is so hard to get at any facts
in Ireland, is that there *are* no facts in Ireland!
This seems to be the opinion of some modern
sceptics in respect of bygone centuries. But
assuredly human nature and human life were not
so very different then and now :—

> "Sunt hic etiam sua praemia laudi :
> Sunt lacrimae rerum ; et mentem mortalia tangunt"

There is even a sense (as Aristotle observed long
ago) in which the portraiture of poetry and popular
tradition is even truer and more real than that of
serious history [1] ($\phi\iota\lambda o\sigma o\phi\acute{\omega}\tau\epsilon\rho o\nu$ $\kappa\alpha\grave{\iota}$ $\sigma\pi o\upsilon\delta\alpha\iota\acute{o}$-

---

[1] *Poet.* Chapter IX. § 3.

τερον ποίησις ἱστορίας ἔστιν). We do not care
so much, in regard to small details of fact respecting a particular person, to know whether this
identical occurrence took place exactly thus, at
some definite place and time, as though we were
cross-examining a witness in a law-court. But it
is interesting, and often important, to know that
such an occurrence represents the person to us in
an aspect and character that seemed natural and
appropriate to those who knew him as he lived
and moved among them. If these stories do not
always record facts, they depict character, which
is of more consequence.[1]

We may indeed feel thankful that the com-
paratively recent date of Dante, and his connection with some stubbornly attested historical
facts, has hitherto saved the poet himself from
being evaporated into a myth (as has sometimes
been the fate of Beatrice Portinari, who is not
similarly protected by history); otherwise we can
scarcely doubt that the perverse ingenuity of
modern, and especially German, criticism would
have disposed of him long ago. If it were not
for these countervailing considerations to the
contrary, there are ample materials, as such

[1] Most admirable is that pregnant saying of Vico: "In
the poetic fables of a whole nation there is more truth than
in a historic narrative written by one man". I note also the
following in Pattison's *Essays*, lately published: "Truth of
representation is not truth of fact merely, it must be truth
of character and life. A work of fiction may easily be more
valuable than a history" (ii. p. 356).

things are generally managed, for the familiar disintegrating process, and for furnishing a very respectable stock-in-trade for a modern school of Chorizontes or Separatists. Thus the great poem offers plenty of microscopic inconsistencies, dialectic anomalies (as noticed long ago by Machiavelli), minute anachronisms, special usages of words, or peculiar constructions, occurring quite commonly in one *Cantica*, and not found, or scarcely found at all, in the others;[1] there are also strange omissions of striking and most important names, still stranger dispositions of the eternal destiny of some characters presumably still too well known at the supposed time of the composition of the poem for such liberties to be ventured upon, such anomalies moreover exhibiting no definite principle, purpose, or plan. Then, again, is it not almost incredible, if Dante really existed, that not a line of his handwriting can be produced? No trace of it can be shown to exist; not even in the public archives of the city in which he is stated to have held so prominent a position. Once more, is not his very name suspiciously significant, *Dante*, or *Durante*, "the Giver", or "the much enduring" ($\pi o\lambda v\tau\lambda\hat{a}s$)— a point strongly insisted on by all the old Commentators—to say nothing of Alighieri, or Aliger, "the wingèd one," *Che sovra gli altri com' aquila vola*? Amidst so much that is suspicious we may well be thankful that, even

---

[1] See Butler's *Paradiso*, note on viii. 61.

if we may not be allowed to believe anything definite that he ever said or did, yet he himself is still spared to us, at least as a "κωφὸν πρόσωπον", and that he has not been long since dismissed to the limbo of imaginary beings, to the company of Homer—Ὅμηρος, "the Joiner" or "Botcher" of Songs, for so indeed has his name been interpreted[1]—wafted into nonentity by a puff of the higher criticism.[2]

But enough of this—let us come to the point more immediately before us. We will begin with

---

[1] This brilliant suggestion as to the significance of the name is made by Vico, *Scienza Nuova*, L. iii. § 7 (p. 399, Ed. 1744), (*Pruove Filologiche*, etc.), "ὅμηρος *vogliono pur essere detto da* ὁμοῦ '*simul*' *et* εἴρειν '*connectere*' . . . *la qual origine è cotanto lontana e sforzata, quanto è agiata e propria per significare l'Omero nostro, che fu* LEGATORE *ovvero* COMPONITORE DI FAVOLE". The name, he points out further, is similar in significance to *Rapsodi*, i.e. *consarcinatori di canti*. I cannot help adding, as a still more astonishing example of perverse ingenuity (though not bearing on the point in the text), the derivation offered by Boccaccio, *Comento*, i. p. 320, "OMERO—*il quale nome è composto ab* O *che in latino viene a dire* IO, *e* MI *che in latino viene a dire* NON, *ed* ERO *che in latino viene a dire* VEGGIO: *e così tutto insieme viene a dire* 'IO NON VEGGIO'!" In the First Edition (Florence, 1724), the passage reads still more strangely, thus :—"*è composto ab* ὸ *che in latino viene a dire* EGLI, *e* μὴ *che in latino viene a dire* NON, *ed* ὁρᾷ *che in latino viene a dire* VEDE: *e così tutto insieme viene a dire* EGLI NON VEDE." In any case *latino* is very curious.

[2] It has been wittily remarked by a well-known living author, that the upshot of the controversy as to the authorship of the *Iliad* and *Odyssey* appears to be that "they were not written by Homer, but by another gentleman of the same name". (See further Supplementary Notes.)

the *features* of the poet. As to these we are left
in no doubt, since it is known that a cast was
made in plaster from his face after death which
still exists, and from which many copies have
been taken. The existence of such an authentic
and unerring record as this renders us independent of the verbal descriptions of biographers.
By it, as we may say, "he being dead, yet
speaketh", and as we reverently look upon it, we
may exclaim with enthusiastic confidence—if
we may be pardoned for thus using his own
words, which have a more solemn import in the
original—

"Or fu sì fatta la sembianza vostra !"[1]

Besides this, and entirely in accordance with it,
we have the well-known portrait by Giotto in
the Chapel of the Bargello, discovered and copied
(happily before the inevitable restoration or re-
painting took place) by Baron Kirkup, and published from his drawing by the Arundel Society.
Lionardo Aretino, it will be remembered, mentions, as still existing in his day, another portrait,
now unhappily lost, in the Church of Santa Croce,
the position of which he minutely describes.[2]

It is interesting to observe how exactly Boccaccio's description corresponds with the still
existing mask. The face long, the nose aquiline,
the cheek-bones high, the under lip projecting
so much as to slightly push out the upper lip

[1] *Par.* xxxi. 108.   [2] *Sup.* p. 76.

also, . . . the expression always melancholy and thoughtful. Such is Boccaccio's description, and it reads almost like notes taken from the mask itself, as indeed it may possibly have been. The only point which does not strike us as in exact correspondence is the size of the eyes, which Boccaccio says were "large rather than small" (*anzi grossi che piccoli*). But they may have been partially closed after death, and moreover, there is an evident drooping of the lids, and relaxation of the muscles of the face (especially on the left side), which a medical friend pointed out to me, and described as probably the result of slight paralysis. I may add that the same friend assured me that, speaking as a medical man, he had not the slightest doubt whatever that the mask was actually taken from a dead man's face, and if so, there certainly can be no doubt that that dead face was indeed that of Dante. It may also be added that when his bones were discovered in so singular and unexpected a manner in 1865, all the measurements of the skull made by professional surgeons were found to correspond exactly with those of the mask which had been brought from Florence to Ravenna for the purpose of making the comparison.[1] The description of his features by Villani is

[1] See also Nicolucci's Monograph on *Il Cranio di Dante*, especially as confirming Boccaccio's statement respecting the cheek-bones. Also an interesting note in Miss Rossetti's *Shadow of Dante*, p. 31 (Ed. 1871), and my article in the *English Historical Review* for January 1889.

little more than a Latin translation of that of Boccaccio, and that of Manetti a servile copy of the words of Villani. Lionardo goes less into detail, referring his readers to the then still existing portrait in Santa Croce. In reference to the size of the eyes, they may also possibly have changed in appearance in later life from the weakness and injury of sight to which Dante himself refers as due both to excessive sorrow, and also to excessive study. See *Vita Nuova*, Chapters XXIII. and XL., and more particularly *Convito* III. 9, where the symptoms and remedies of this disease of the eyes are explained.

Passing from his *features* to his *stature*, his biographers all agree that he was of moderate height[1] (*mediocre* and *decente*[2] are the terms used), but when I say they agree, it is only the agreement of those who evidently copy one

---

[1] It should be noticed that one of the traditional and anonymous anecdotes about Dante describes him as *molto piccolo*. This is apparently stated or invented quite unnecessarily, to give point to the jest. Dante is said to have been taunted as being like the letter I. [This might imply that he was *magro*, but would not justify the gloss that he was *molto piccolo*.] To this taunt he is said to have made the rather laboured reply that he could not say that his opponent was of so much importance as the previous letter [*i.e.* H, which, though bulky in form, counts for *nothing* in pronunciation], but that he was just equal to the following letter twice over [*i.e.* K K, or Ca-Ca, *i.e.* a fool].

[2] As Tacitus says of Agricola, *habitus . . . decentior quam sublimior fuit* (C. xliv.).

original, viz. Boccaccio. Boccaccio also states that he stooped in his gait, especially in his later years, and that to such an extent as to give the impression that he was slightly hump-backed. In the Commentary on *Inf.* viii. 1 (*Lezione* 33) he repeats this statement, with the addition that he knew intimately Andrea Poggi, son of Leon Poggi, and his wife, who was a sister of Dante. This Andrea, he adds, marvellously resembled Dante in his features and also in his figure, and so walked with a slightly humped back (*e così andava un poco gobbo*), as Dante is said to have done. It would perhaps be scarcely in point to refer to *Purg.* xix. 40-2, where Dante from a temporary cause attributes to himself a curved and stooping figure—

> "Seguendo lui, portava la mia fronte
> Come colui che l' ha di pensier carca,
> Che fa di sè un mezzo arco di ponte"—

except indeed so far that the result in actual life may have been due to this same cause, he being one who was habitually *melancolico e pensoso*.

As to his beard and the colour of his hair there is some little doubt. The biographers all attribute to him thick, black and slightly curly hair, but we have some suspicion that they do so to give point to the story (generally repeated in connection with that description) of the old gossips of Verona noticing that he bore upon him the marks of his visit to Hell in his dark colour (*colore bruno*) and his frizzled black hair.[1] Certain it is at any rate that Dante himself applies the term *flavus, i.e.* light brown, yellow, or fair, to the colour of his own hair in youth. See *Ecl.* i. 1. 42—

> "Nonne triumphales melius pexare capillos,
> Et patrio, redeam si quando, abscondere canos
> Fronde sub inserta *solitum flavescere*, Sarno."

"And if I should return to my native Arno ever, hide beneath a wreath of leaves my grey hairs, I who once was fair."

Compare with this, at any rate so far as relates to the greyness of his hairs, the pathetic commencement of *Par.* xxv. 7—

> "*con altro vello*
> Ritornerò poeta, ed in sul fonte
> Del mio battesmo prenderò il cappello."

The *altro vello* seems to refer to the changed colour of his hair since the days when *dormiò agnello nel bello ovile.* Unfortunately the picture by Giotto does not help us as to this point, since the hair is concealed by a closely fitting cap. He appears according to the biographers to have worn a beard,[2] but if so, it is very strange that this

---

[1] Boccaccio adds that Dante overheard this, and was both pleased and amused to think that the old ladies really believed it (*conoscendo che da pura credenza delle donne* [le parole] *veniano* (*Vita, c.* VIII.).

[2] At first sight one might be tempted to quote *Purg.* xxxi. 68, where Beatrice bids Dante *alza la barba*, but it is explained immediately afterwards that the word is used metaphorically to indicate maturity of age.

> "E quando per la barba *il viso* chiese
> Ben conobbi il velen dell' argomento."   ll. 74-5.

never appears in any representation, of him. Boccaccio says that his beard as well as his hair was
thick, dark, and frizzled (*spessi, neri, e crespi*); "*spissa
barba*," repeats Villani. So also Manetti (*capillis
et barba prolixis, nigris subcrispisque*); while,
according to Filelfo, he was *barbatus óptime.*[1]

All seem agreed that his gait and movements
were slow and dignified, as befitting both the
countenance and the character of the man. *Il suo
andare,* says Boccaccio, *fu grave e mansueto.*[2]
And so, in slightly varying language, the other
biographers, till we come to the imaginative
Filelfo, who always clothes his hero with all
qualities that he thinks admirable or desirable,
even if they do not happen to be consistent.
Erat Dante, he says, *proceritatis personae,
celeritatis agilitatisque totius plenus, i.e.* Dante
had a tall figure, and was full of the utmost
rapidity of movement and agility! Yet he adds,
incesso gravissimo, "with the most solemn or
dignified gait"! Which of these statements are
we to accept? Did Filelfo really imagine Dante
advancing to an object "with leaps and bounds"?
It is commonly said that persons of a certain
character which I need not particularise more
definitely should have good memories. But it is

---

[1] In Boccaccio's *Vita*, c. 3, it is mentioned as one of the
effects of Dante's grief for the loss of Beatrice that he became
"*magro,* BARBUTO, *e quasi tutto transformato,*" etc.

[2] This would be illustrated by *Purg.* iii. 10, 11—

> "Quando li piedi suoi lasciar la fretta,
> Che l'onestade ad ogni atto dismaga."

scarcely less important that they should be furnished with some slight sense of dramatic propriety.

So again, while early writers attribute to him a grave and thoughtful, and even melancholy, countenance (Boccaccio), not inconsistent, however, with affability (*comitas*), as Villani adds, or with his expression being pleasing (*gratus*), according to Lionardo, Filelfo boldly improves upon them all by saying that "his countenance was always grave and cheerful (*vultu semper gravi ac hilari*!), and that it was one that made every one that saw him love him"! If so, the majority of men concealed their love only too effectually.

We have little doubt that Dante is describing his own habits and demeanour when he writes thus in the *Convito* (iii. 8): "The soul reveals itself in the mouth (he has already stated that it does so in the eyes) like colour behind glass. . . . It is then becoming in a man, in order to reveal his soul in tempered cheerfulness, to laugh moderately,[1] with a noble severity, and without much movement of the limbs. . . . Thus the Book of the Four Cardinal Virtues [2] commands us: 'Thy smile should be without laughter, and thy voice should not cackle like a hen'." We feel sure that Dante is bitterly thinking of his experience of the vulgar hilarity which he was often compelled to witness at the courts of his patrons. How distasteful to

[1] Dante has described one of his own "moderate laughs" in *Purg.* iv. 121-2 :—

> "Gli atti suoi pigri, e le corte parole
>   Mosson le labbra mie *un poco* a riso."

[2] Attributed in Dante's time to Seneca.

him this was, and how very little pains he took to conceal that it was so, is exhibited in many traditional anecdotes.

In connection with some of the characteristics already mentioned, we are not surprised to find that he was taciturn ("*taciturnior quam loquacior,*" Filelfo), and that when he did speak he spoke slowly and with deliberation, but very keenly to the point, especially in his retorts, as again several anecdotes testify. As we read in Lionardo, he was *parlatore rado e tardo, ma nelle sue risposte molto sottile.* Or as Boccaccio says, *Rade volte, se non domandato, parlava . . . non pertanto là dove si richiedeva eloquentissimo e facondo, e con ottima e pronta prolazione.* (He seldom spoke unless he was spoken to; when, however, occasion arose, he was most eloquent and fluent, and had an excellent and ready delivery.)

Does not Dante again seem to us to be drawing his own portrait when he describes the stately and dignified denizens of the *nobile castello* in Limbo, those mighty spirits whom even to have seen ennobles him—

> " Spiriti magni
> Che del vederli in me stesso n'esalto " ?

Thus he describes them—

> " Genti v' eran, con occhi tardi e gravi,
>   Di grande autorità ne' lor sembianti :
>   Parlavan rado, con voci soavi."[1]

[1] *Inf.* iv. 112-14.

Or again, in the sympathetic portrait of the shade
of Sordello—

> "Come ti stavi altera e disdegnosa,
> E nel muover degli occhi onesta e tarda."[1]

We are also forcibly reminded of some of the
minor details of Aristotle's portraiture of the High-
Souled Man (μεγαλόψυχος), just as there is much
in Dante's recorded sayings and actions that
recall the more important features of that ideal
character, *e.g.* κίνησις βραδεῖα τοῦ μεγαλοψύχου
δοκεῖ εἶναι, καὶ φωνὴ βαρεῖα, καὶ λέξις στά-
σιμος.

A minor point noticed by his biographers,
though not, if I remember rightly, by Boccaccio,
is Dante's punctilious neatness in his dress. He
was distinguished, according to Villani, *vestitu
honesto sed perpolito.* He adds that he often
was seen in public wearing a "tabard," *tabarro
contectus.* The tabard was a short cape, but I
cannot find from other references to it that any
special character, either of luxury or otherwise,
was attached to the wearing of it. Villani
probably mentions it simply as a fact, which had
perhaps survived in men's memories. Lionardo
says that Dante was *uomo molto pulito,* and
Manetti states that before his exile he was
dressed becomingly, but not too showily, in a
way entirely suited to a man of such great
dignity.

But before we pass on to trace the " qualities

---

[1] *Purg.* vi. 62, 63.

and defects ", as Boccaccio styles them, of his
character, there are two other points on which it
occurs to me to say a few words—his handwriting,
and his love of music and painting.

As to his handwriting, it is a most curious
and almost incredible fact that not a trace of it
remains.   Considering his important public offices
at Florence, we should certainly have expected
to find his handwriting somewhere among her
official documents.   The most diligent researches
in those archives have failed to discover even
his signature anywhere.   Considering again that
his fame sprang to an almost incredible height
immediately after his death, that several Commentaries were written on the *Divina Commedia*
within ten years of his death, it is nothing less
than astonishing that every line of the autographs
of his numerous works, already and at once held
in such esteem, should have totally disappeared.
Was there no one found among his many
admirers—we might almost say worshippers—to
treasure even a fragment of such precious relics,
then surely easily accessible,

> " And dying, mention it within their wills,
>   Bequeathing it as a rich legacy
>   Unto their issue " ?

Still more strange does this seem when we
remember that not only does Boccaccio state that
at any rate several of Dante's Epistles were still
extant (*delle quali ancora appariscono assai*),

but that even Lionardo Aretino, who died 1444, was familiar with several autograph letters of Dante, and consequently is enabled in a very interesting passage to describe his handwriting minutely, and, as far as we can judge, with every appearance of accurate truth. This is what he says : " He wrote a very beautiful hand (*fu scrittore perfetto*); his writing was thin and long, and very correctly formed (*magra e lunga e molto corretta*), secondo io ho veduto (note these words) *in alcune pistole di sua propria mano scritte.*" It will be recollected also that Lionardo twice refers to a letter of Dante's (now lost) respecting the battle of Campaldino, from which he quotes some sentences *verbatim;* wherein Dante describes his own terror when he first found himself (as we should say) " under fire." Lionardo mentions that it also contained a plan of the battle. So that at least a century after Dante's death some of these precious documents were still preserved. We cannot help noting how intrinsically probable is Lionardo's description of the deliberate, precise, and beautifully accurate hand, which we should antecedently have felt certain that Dante would have written. If there is any connection between character and handwriting, I feel quite sure that Dante was not σπευστικός (or apt to be in a hurry) in this or any other respects, but that he formed all his letters carefully, and no doubt dotted his *i*'s.

Filelfo in the main repeats Lionardo, but adds

that Dante was particularly correct as to spelling (*orthographiam tenebat ad unguem*), "so far as it was possible for any one to be who was not acquainted with Greek"!

It is curious that by an accident Dante's father's autograph has been preserved in the signature to a transfer of a piece of land (*petia terrae*) dated September 29, 1239, which he witnessed or executed as *imperiali auctoritate judex atque notarius*. This curious document, formerly in the Monastery of Monte Oliveto, and now in the State Archives at Florence, is reprinted, and the facsimile of the autograph reproduced in the Monograph entitled *Casa di Dante* (1865), pp. 13 and 25.[1]

Next as to Dante's love of music and painting. Boccaccio says that in his youth he was extremely devoted to music and singing, that he himself composed, and that he became intimate with all of his contemporaries who most excelled in these arts. So also say Villani and Manetti. The same thing is frequently implied in the current traditions, and is fully attested by numerous passages in the *Divina Commedia*. No reader can fail to have been struck by the frequency of comparisons and illustrations drawn from music in the *Purgatorio* and *Para-diso*, and the evident delight with which such

---

[1] There is indeed a document preserved, dated Padua, August 27, 1306, to the execution of which Dante himself is mentioned as a witness ; but it does not appear that he actually signed it in that capacity.

recollections of "the concord of sweet sounds"
are introduced.   All will remember the charming
episode of Casella in *Purg.* ii., and how the spirits
in the Ante-Purgatorio incurred the displeasure
of Cato by lingering in wrapt enchantment (*tutti
fissi ed attenti*) to the sweet strains of Casella.
We also observe how often Dante is arrested by
the exquisite melody of the penitent souls singing the Church hymns and offices,[1] so sweetly
indeed that no words could describe it (*Purg.*
xii. 111), and that he was transported out of himself thereby (viii. 15).   Then there are very frequent metaphors and comparisons drawn from
music, *e.g.* voices singing with the accompaniment
of the organ (*Purg.* ix. 144), or with that of the
harp (*Par.* xx. 142-4); organ music by itself
(*Par.* xvii. 44); the viol (*giga*) and harp (*Par.*
xiv. 118); the lute and the shawm or bagpipes
(*Par.* xx. 22-4); several voices singing in harmony (*Par.* vi. 124, viii. 17), the chiming of
church bells (*Par.* x. 139, etc.); besides very
many passages, too numerous to quote, in which
the exquisite beauty of the heavenly music
generally is over and over again referred to,[2] in
comparison of which (as he says in one place)
the sweetest melody ever heard on this earth
would be as harsh as a thunder-clap (*Par.* xxiii.
97-100).   Finally, in *Conv.* ii. 14, the utterly
absorbing effect of music on men (*sicchè quasi*

[1] e.g. *Purg.* ix. 141, xii. 111;   *Par.* xxiii. 128-9.
[2] e.g. *Par.* x. 70-81, xxvii. 3.

cessano da ogni operazione) is described in language very like that of *Purg.* ii. 117, where the Spirits hearing Casella's strains are

" si contenti
Come a nessun toccasse altro la mente " ;

also like that of line 108 of the same Canto, where Dante refers to the soothing effect of Casella's music on his own often troubled mind when they were still living together on earth.

All this very amply justifies the statement of his biographers as to Dante's devotion to music. They do not, I think, say much as to his love of the sister art of painting, except that Lionardo explicitly states *di sua mano egregiamente disegnava*, but we have Dante's own direct testimony in a well-known and very beautiful passage of the *V. N.* c. 35 : " On that day which fulfilled the year since my lady had been made one of the citizens of the eternal life, remembering me of her as I sat alone, I was drawing an angel on certain tablets, and while I was thus drawing, I turned my eyes and I saw a vision " (which is then described). And after the vision had departed, " I returned to my occupation, that is, the drawing of figures of angels." This throws light on the minuteness and artistic feeling with which those pictured scenes on the pavement and the walls of the *Cornici* of the Mountain of Purgatory are imagined and described, such as no master of pencil or of graving-tool on earth ever traced (see *Purg.* xii. 64, etc.); such that not only Polycletus but even Nature's self had been shamed thereby (*Purg.* x. 32-3). Other passages interesting in this connection are (*a*) the reference to a painter painting with his model before him (*Purg.* xxxii. 67) :—

> "Come pittor che con esemplo pinga
> Disegnerei," etc.

and (β), in contrast with this, the description of God as the painter who needs no such help, in reference to the representation of the Eagle's head by the glorified spirits in Jupiter :—

> "Quei che dipinge lì non ha chi il guidi." [1]

Moreover, according to tradition, a friendship existed between Dante and Giotto similar to that which (as we have seen above) he cultivated with the chief musicians of his day. This is mentioned by Benvenuto da Imola and by Vasari,[2] the former telling a curious anecdote of a conversation between Dante and Giotto while the latter was painting in Arena Chapel, and a witty repartee of his which he says pleased Dante extremely. We all of course remember how Dante illustrates the transient character of human fame by the example of Giotto so rapidly eclipsing Cimabue :—

---

[1] *Par.* xviii. 109.

[2] The fact that Giotto more than once painted Dante makes this friendship probable. The story referred to in the text must not be relied upon, since it is as old as Macrobius, as indeed Benvenuto was aware (see Com. on *Purg.* xi. 95, vol. iii. p. 313)

" Credette Cimabue nella pittura
    Tener lo campo, ed ora ha Giotto il grido,
    Sì che la fama di colui è oscura." [1]

Also another illustration of the same sentiment
is drawn a few lines before from another branch
of the painter's art, viz. that of illumination
(*alluminare*), in which Oderisi, the glory of Gubbio
(*L'onor d' Agobbio*), has been rapidly supplanted
by Franco of Bologna (*Purg.* xi. 79-84).

We must not omit to quote the very striking
sentiment in the Canzone to Trattato iv. of
the *Convito*—

    " Poi chi pinge figura
        Se non può esser lei non la può porre."

This is thus explained in the commentary in
c. 10: "No painter could produce any figure
unless by a mental effort (*intenzionalmente*) he can
himself become that which the figure ought to
be." A most true and profound sentiment. It
is thus admirably illustrated by Dr. Witte: "Fra
Angelico could not paint the fiery glow of passion,
nor Michael Angelo the glory of devout resigna-
tion." [2] Aristotle has pointed out the same truth
in the *Poetics*, c. 17, but I do not remember that
Dante, with all his minute and extensive knowledge of Aristotle, ever refers to that work.

Finally, I must not omit to quote that most
beautiful illustration from art (though the reference need not be limited to the painter's art

[1] *Inf.* xi. 94-6.
[2] Quoted by Dean Plumptre, ii. p. 284.

alone), where Dante explains how all the pro-
ductions of Nature fall short of the Divine ideal
of perfection, for Nature's works are like those of
an artist who has the feeling of his art, but a
faltering hand :—

> "Similemente operando all' artista,
> Ch' ha l' abito dell' arte, e man che trema."

Turning now from these more or less external
characteristics to traits of character, or, as Boccaccio calls them, " qualities and defects of Dante,"
the first point that would perhaps strike any one,
as it certainly struck his early biographers, was
the habit of *self-assertion*, which by some is represented simply as pride or arrogance, while
others, in designating it as μεγαλοψυχία, or
high-mindedness, seem to our modern notions
to palliate it perhaps rather than justify it.

If we first collect the principal facts on which
the charge is based, we shall better be able to
judge of the character of the charge itself.   First
Boccaccio says that Dante was of a disposition
alto e disdegnoso molto, but having given as
an illustration of this his proud refusal to return
to Florence,[2] much as he longed to do so, on any
humiliating conditions, he exclaims : " O noble
scorn of a high-souled man," etc.—so that at
least is not a form of pride for censure.   Boccaccio
goes on to state that Dante's contemporaries report

---

[1] *Par.* xiii. 77-8.
[2] Chapter xii.   See also chapter viii. *sub fin.*

that his opinion of himself was fully on a level
with his actual superiority, and an illustration of
this is found in the well-known story of the
embassy to Boniface (" If I go, who remains ? and
if I remain, who goes ? "), which, as we know,
gave the deepest offence at Florence. We are all
familiar with the passages in the *Divina Commedia* where the author speaks with magnificent
self-confidence as to the greatness and immortality
of his work,—" magnificent," I say, because most
amply justified by the verdict of posterity. With
splendid audacity he ranks himself among the six
great poets of the world (*Inf.* iv. 102)[1]; but *we*
feel that that class might be much further reduced in number before we began to think about
striking out *his* name. We remember how, in
conversing with Cacciaguida (*Par.* xvii. 115-20),
he hesitates between the present odium of utter-
ing the bitter things which truth demanded, and
the risk, if he fails to do so, of his work not living " among those who will call these times
ancient ". Also how—with that curious colloca-
tion of the sublime and the homely (this very
contrast being often δι' ὕβριν, as Aristotle
would say) which so frequently startles us in
Dante—he makes Cacciaguida reply that he must
tell the whole truth without any reserve, and " let
those that itch scratch." I scarcely venture to
adduce in this relation *Purg.* xi. 97-9, since it is
not at all certain (though I think it is most

---

[1] Compare Horace, *Carm.* iii. 30, especially line 14, " Sume
superbiam Quæsitam meritis ".

likely) that Dante himself is intended by the one who shall perchance displace both the Guidos from their poetic supremacy.

In this connection I may perhaps mention two or three passages embodying Dante's opinion of the female sex generally, which must be admitted to breathe a somewhat intolerant and contemptuous spirit, not unmixed with a certain amount of bitterness, which is scarcely of favourable omen for the smoothness of his relations with his own wife Gemma. The worst passage, I think, is that which occurs in the *Quaestio de Aqua*, etc., Chapter XIX., where he cuts short rather a technical and difficult argument by saying that, " it must now be clear even to women " (*sicut manifestum esse potest etiam mulieribus*). There is a good deal of bitterness in his reference to the transgression of Eve in *Purg.* xxix. 24-30, where he speaks almost as if smarting under a personal injury at her hands. The first vision of the earthly Paradise caused him to reproach the hardihood of Eve, because " when heaven and earth were all obedience, a woman alone, and she but lately formed, could not endure to remain under any veil; under which had she devoutly remained, I should have tasted these ineffable delights long since, and for a long season ".[1] There is again something a little comic in the evident satisfaction with which (in the *De Vulg. Eloq.* I. iv.), when speaking of the origin of language, he notes that it was woman,

[1] Compare *Purg.* xxxii. 31-2.

not man, who is recorded in Genesis as having first broken silence in the newly-created world. " It is found," he says, "at the beginning of Genesis that a woman, in fact the most presumptuous Eve, spoke first before all others, when she replied to the devil, who was questioning her, ' We may eat of the fruit of the trees of the garden,' etc. At the same time," adds Dante solemnly, "though in the actual record woman is found to have spoken first, it is reasonable for us to believe that man spoke first; and it is suitable to suppose that so noble an act of the human race as speech should have first proceeded from a man rather than a woman " :[1]

Though I have no wish to defend the spirit implied in such passages as these, I must say a few words on the general subject of what I may

[1] It has sometimes been observed that Dante never regards the mother in any other light than that of a nurse (and very beautiful indeed are some of the passages in which he does so), never as though having any share in parental authority. It is remarkable that in *Conv.* iv. 24, quoting Col. iii. 20, he substitutes *padri* for *parentes* : " *Figliuoli, ubbidite alli vostri* PADRI *per tutte cose*" ; and he proceeds to consider the modifications in this command required if the father be dead, or if he had died without appointing a guardian to his children ; but among several possible substitutes for paternal authority he never mentions the mother. Shortly before, in the same chapter, when quoting Prov. i. 8 to prove that obedience is the special virtue of youth, he gives only the first clause, " My son, hear the instruction of thy father," omitting " and forsake not the law of thy mother ". These may seem " straws ", but they still may show how the wind blows.

call the *vulgar* charge of self-assertion, as alleged
against Dante and some other great men in whom
the habit has been conspicuous. When we read
of the self-assertion and self-confidence of such
men as Pericles, Dante, Pitt; or observe it in the
ideal sketch of Aristotle's μεγαλόψυχος, we are
apt to forget that we are dealing with the cases
of *altogether exceptional men,* with the cases not of
one man in a thousand, or even in a million, but
with such men as arise only once in the whole
world in the lapse of many generations. Consequently any judgment based on the experience
of ordinary men must necessarily be utterly at
fault. True humility does not consist in a conscious self-depreciation. If it did, it would be
very difficult to distinguish it from hypocrisy.
Granting, however, the case of such an excep-
tionally great man as I have supposed, one who
cannot help feeling his real greatness and power,
one whose consciousness of his greatness has been
amply justified, and more than ratified by the
judgment and admiration of mankind, can we be
surprised if such a man claims a position for himself, and employs language about himself which
would be in any ordinary man exaggerated,
offensive, and intolerable ? (οὐκ ἄτοπον . . . .
εἰ μὴ ἀληθεύσεται κατ᾽ αὐτοῦ τὸ ὕπαρχον;[1])
The cases in question are, *ex hypothesi,* quite out
of the range of our ordinary experience, and

---

[1] Ar. *Nic. Eth.* I. x. 7.

therefore not to be judged by it. They are, as Dante says,

"Per modo tutto fuor del modern' uso."[1]

We may apply to such cases of self-assertion the language of Aristotle in respect of some of the bold anomalies in Homer: "They would be quite intolerable if any ordinary poet were to venture upon them."[2] I am not saying that this habit of self-assertion is even in these great men a lovable habit, or a praiseworthy one, but it is natural, and almost inevitable, and certainly not a matter for censure in the way it is often censured.[3] Even so humble and gentle a spirit as Wordsworth spoke with almost Dantesque confidence of the immortality of his own work; but this (as Principal Shairp says) "is not vanity, but the calm confidence of a man who feels the rock under his feet, and who knows that he is in harmony with the everlasting truth of things." It was remarked by a distinguished man not long ago: "One of the absurdities of the English character at the present day is that no one has an estimate of his own intrinsic value."[4]

Under any circumstances, however, let it certainly not be forgotten that this μεγαλοψυχία is by no means incompatible with true humility.

---

[1] *Purg.* xvi. 42.

[2] *Poetics*, xxiv. § 10.

[3] As Tacitus says of autobiography, it often argues " fiduciam potius morum quam arrogantiam," *Agric.* i.

[4] Lord Dalling, quoted in Hayward's *Essays*, ii. p. 338.

Nor was it so in Dante's case. For I doubt not
that in the following passages he spoke with the
same utter sincerity as in those in which we find
him asserting himself so uncompromisingly. For
instance, (1) in his Epistle [1] to the Cardinals at
Carpentras, assembled in conclave after the death
of Clement V., he describes himself as "among
the lambs of the flock of Jesus Christ, one of the
most insignificant." There is surely a touch of
quiet humour in the way in which he proceeds
to defend himself for his apparent presumption,
under these circumstances, in addressing the Cardinals at all ; thus, as it were, like Uzzah, daring
to put forth his hand to steady the tottering ark.
"No," he says, "I am not guilty of the sin of Uzzah.
I am not interfering with the ark, but only with
the refractory oxen (*boves calcitrantes*), that are
dragging it out of the path"! One wonders how
the Cardinals relished that ingenious distinction.
(2) In the *Quaestio de Aqua et Terra*, already
quoted (one of his very last works, and dated
within a few months of his death), he introduces
himself as "Dante Alighieri of Florence... among
true philosophers the least" (*inter vere philoso-
phantes minimus*). (3) Again, in the very first
chapter of the *Convito*, while offering the "instruction of knowledge" to those who in their
ignorance are still "filling themselves with the
husks that the swine do eat," he adds, "Not that
I myself sit at that blessed table, but having

[1] *Ep.* ix. § 5.

escaped the pasture of the vulgar herd, I gather
up, at the feet of those who sit there, some of the
crumbs which fall from them." This reminds
us of the modesty so beautifully expressed by
Wordsworth in "The Poet's Epitaph":—

> " Contented if he might enjoy
> The things which others understand."

(4) The same keynote of humility is struck at
the very end of the *Convito*, in the last chapter (iv.
30): " Every good workman," he says, "at the end
of his work, ought to ennoble and embellish it as
much as he can, so that it may leave his hands
more famous and more precious. This I propose
to do here, not as though I were a good workman,
but as an imitator of those that are." (5) Lastly,
we may add the language of the no longer extant
letter of Dante, quoted by Lionardo Aretino,
where he refers to the disasters flowing to him
from his own Priorate at Florence—" of which
office," he says, "though in wisdom I was not
worthy, yet in loyalty and maturity of age I was
not unworthy."

Most remarkable, too, is the frequent homage
which Dante pays to the Virtue of Humility.
There is no virtue for which he shows a more
enthusiastic admiration. He attributes it over
and over again to Beatrice, in the *Vita Nuova*, as
though it were her most glorious and distin-
guishing attribute. " At the sound of her voice
all sweetness and every humble thought arises in
the heart" (Sonnet xi. c. 21). When he sees

her in vision lying dead, there was in her such
humility as seemed to say, "I am in peace"
(Canzone ii. c. 23). "When she went abroad
she was clothed with humility" (see Sonnet xv.
c. 26, and compare c. 1). "It was by reason of
her marvellous humility that the Eternal Lord
called her so early to heaven (Canzone iii. c. 32),
and when he called her there, he placed her "in
the heaven of humility where Mary is" (Sonnet
xviii. c. 35).

Dante intended to devote the last of the fourteen projected Trattati of the *Convito* to the
subject of Pride, "which," as he says, "often
makes even our virtues less beautiful and less
attractive," and meanwhile urges us to study
that part of philosophy where she is an example
of humility, namely, moral philosophy. Finally,
in that splendid hymn to the Virgin with which
the last Canto of the *Paradiso* opens, St. Bernard
addresses her as

"Umile ed alta più che creatura."

In justice to Dante, then, such passages as
these must not be forgotten, though one does not
find them quoted like the others, by which the
vulgar charge of arrogance is sustained. Consequently this is an aspect of his character that is
commonly overlooked.[1]

[1] It is not a little remarkable, too, how he shrinks from
mentioning his own name, not only in the *Commedia* (with
one well-known exception), but also in his other works, and
notably in the *De Vulg. Eloq.*, where he several times quotes
his own *Canzoni*, but always as the words of the friend of
Cino da Pistoia (*amicus ejus*).

Another fault with which his biographers commonly charge him is that of inordinate ambition and love of praise, "beyond what was becoming in so serious a philosopher" (Manetti). Villani says that he was undeniably *avidissimus aurae popularis cupidusque gloriae et honoris*, though this was well directed in his case towards poetry. So, again, Boccaccio, *Vaghissimo fu d'onore e di pompa*, perhaps, as he adds, to a degree unsuitable to so great a man. But he proceeds to palliate this by declaring that it was, as Aristotle says, ἐπ' ἀρετῇ, and he thinks that it was the extreme rareness of excellence in poetry that made him specially wish to be distinguished in it. In this noblest sense of ambition alone—*laudari a laudatis viris*—is the charge (if such it be) true. The only solid fact to which the biographers commit themselves is his earnest desire for the poet's laurel crown at Florence. I do not find any trace of the vulgar ambition which loves the praise of man as such, and from any source. Dante assuredly was not prone to what A. H. Clough describes as "the horrible pleasure of pleasing inferior people" (*Amours de Voyage*, xi.). I feel sure that of Dante, as of Aristotle's ideal, it could be truly said—Τῆς δε τιμῆς παρὰ τῶν τυχόντων καὶ ἐπὶ μικροῖς πάμπαν ὀλιγωρήσει (*Nic. Eth.* IV. iii. 17).

He is also said, and no doubt with truth, to have had a very sharp and biting tongue. His biographers agree as to this, and the belief has been very abundantly reflected and exemplified in cur-

rent traditions. If some of these be true, he spared
neither friend nor foe,[1] and in his repartees he
was, as Lionardo says, *molto sottile.* It is not
merely that his words had the "*sapor di forte
agrume*" of which he himself speaks in his conversation with Cacciaguida (*Par.* xvii. 117), but they
exhibit that peculiar form of quiet, subtle, and very
refined, and therefore very biting, irony of which
Heinrich Heine was so conspicuous a master.

I have not space to quote any of these anecdotes, but I will give one instance from the
Divina Commedia. It occurs in *Par.* xxxi. 37-9.
Dante explains how natural it was that he should
be utterly bewildered with the startling change
when he first found himself in the highest heaven.
"I who had come from the human to the divine;
from time to eternity; and *from Florence to a
people just and sane.*" It is impossible to surpass
the keenness of satire which treats that last
thought as the climax of all. It has also the
element of ἀπροσδόκητον or surprise, which strikes
us so often in Heine's most effective thrusts.[2]

One story which would illustrate both of the

---

[1] Like the μεγαλόψυχος once more, he was παρρησιάστης διὰ
τὸ καταφρονεῖν, or as Tacitus says of Agricola (c. xxii.)—
"honestius putabat offendisse quam odisse."

[2] Compare the following from Heine : "It is curious that
the three greatest adversaries of Napoleon have all of them
ended miserably. Castlereagh cut his own throat ; Louis
XVIII. rotted upon his throne ; and Professor Saalfeld is still
a professor at Göttingen."—(Quoted by M. Arnold, *Essays
in Criticism*, p. 173.)

qualities noticed, arrogance and sharpness of speech, may be quoted, as it is very brief. A buffoon had received from his patrons, as a mark of approbation of his talents, a very handsome robe, which he displayed with pride to Dante as being more than he had ever earned for himself by all his books. "True indeed," said Dante, "and the reason is that you have met with your likes, but I have not yet met with mine." [1]

We have now to deal with the more serious charge that has been commonly made against Dante, of licentiousness, and that prolonged even to old age. Now, first of all, when we say " commonly made", it is to be remembered that it comes to little more than saying that the charge is made by Boccaccio. The other biographies are not independent voices, but mere echoes, and some of them, rather like a certain celebrated Irish echo, repeat a good deal more than was uttered by the original voice. This, as we have seen, is notably the case with the so-called *Compendio* of Boccaccio, and with the exception of Manetti [2] (who is generally only Boccaccio in a

---

[1] I am afraid this story, like many of the others associated with Dante by anonymous tradition, will not bear investigation. Papanti notes (p. 95) that it is also told of Michael Savonarola (grandfather of Girolamo), and of Marco Lombardo (for whom see *Purg.* xvi.).

[2] Manetti, while admitting Dante to have been "lascivis aliquantulum amoribus obnoxius," apologises for him on two grounds, (1) that this was due "potius gratiosae hominis naturae quam cuidam gravissimi viri levitati," and (2) that Socrates before him was open to the same charge.

Latin dress), there is very little to be found about this charge in the other biographers. The question then really comes to this : What is the value of Boccaccio's statement, and on what grounds is he likely to have made it ? The statement itself, often quoted and often discussed, is this : "Amidst such great virtue, and such great wisdom as we have shown to have existed in this marvellous poet, licentiousness held very ample sway (*truovò ampissimo luogo la lussuria*), and that not only in his younger years, but even in mature life." Boccaccio solemnly apologises for this failure, which he considers *naturale e comune e quasi necessario* by the example of many famous characters in sacred and profane history (such as Jupiter, Hercules, Paris, David, Solomon, and Herod), coming to the general conclusion that "our poet, being not excused by, but accused in such good company, need not hang his head so low as if his case were an exceptional one"! The offensive details will not be forgotten with which this general charge is amplified by the author of the *Compendio*, the *pargoletta* of Lucca, and the pretty Alpine girl with a goître, and so forth ! [1]

[1] Ch. xii. As a further illustration how such a charge "vires acquirit eundo" we may cite the anonymous *Teleutologia*, for which see *sup.* p. 89 : "Haec illa [luxuria] est quae Dantem Alighierii . . . naturae dotibus coruscantem et omnium morum habitus rutilantem, *adulterinis amplexibus renenavit*" ! [quoted by Macrì-Leone, p. cxv]. For the particular case mentioned in the text, of the "Lucchese, . . . la quale *egli nomina* (!) Pargoletta," etc., see the origin of the myth explained, *sup.* p. 12.

Confining ourselves then to the original language of the genuine *Vita* of Boccaccio, let us try to estimate its actual value.

(1) It is obvious to remark in the first place that Boccaccio cannot in this case be speaking from personal knowledge ; for, however knowing and precocious he may have been in such matters, he was only eight years old when Dante died, and he wrote nearly half a century later. This however cannot be pressed too far, since it applies to anything else that is stated by Boccaccio, and he had at any rate ample opportunities for obtaining information.

(2) While I do not charge Boccaccio (like Filelfo) with deliberate and baseless invention, yet I suspect that he allowed his fancy to play rather freely around any nucleus of fact, or what he took for fact, that he might have to start upon.

(3) Though it is impossible now either to prove or disprove that Boccaccio had obtained definite information on this point by inquiry (for he never asserts this in respect of this charge as he does in regard to various other statements made by him from time to time),[1] yet I strongly suspect

---

[1] It is not a little remarkable that in his Commentary (his latest work) Boccaccio, though commenting at inordinate length on the moral significance of the *tre fiere* in *Inf.* i. (*lussuria, superbia, avarizia*), merely says quite vaguely—
"POTERONO *questi vizi essere all' autore in singolarità cagione di resistenza e di paura*" (Lezione vi.), see pp. 178, 185. At the same time a few pages further on (p. 188) the charge is more definitely made, though somewhat incidentally.

that the supposed "nucleus of fact" in this case was presented by the language of Dante's own self-accusation [1] in the expressions of reproach, which he puts into the mouth of Beatrice in *Purg.* xxx.[2]

(4) The biographers themselves contain some countervailing statements which go far to disprove or modify the accusation in question. So far as an *argumentum e silentio* goes, it may be observed that the only really contemporary writer who has described Dante's character and habits,

---

[1] We have perhaps other instances of the habit of drawing such ill-founded inferences in the cases noticed *sup.* pp. 20, 29.

[2] The discussion of the meaning of that remarkable scene would carry us far beyond our present limits, and I must not embark upon it. I will only make two remarks : (1) It is most unsafe to take in strict literalness all that people say when describing themselves as "miserable sinners," especially in the case of one who has a very high ideal of his duty or calling, and one too, who has the habit (to us now scarcely intelligible) of expressing the simplest facts in the language of more than Oriental metaphor. I do not mean that here, or, in any case, Dante flung about his words at random, but his exceedingly sensitive nature may have led to overstatement of his failings as judged by the language of ordinary men. (2) We find more than once in the *Convito* strong protests by Dante himself against the misunderstanding of his language when he employs such metaphors as *amore, donna,* etc., the danger of which he seems distinctly to have anticipated. I will only quote one sample. In *Convito* iii. 3 he says that a certain expression which he has used " will show that this ' love ' is that which arises in the noblest natures, viz. the love of truth and of virtue, and will exclude any false opinion about me, by the which it might be suspected that my love is associated with the pleasures of sense." (Compare also *Convito,* iv. 1 *fin.*)

viz. G. Villani, in his *Cronica* (ix. 136), says nothing on this subject, though he does charge Dante with self-assertion and arrogant treatment of others, qualities, however, which he says are more than counterbalanced by his learning and other virtues. Boccaccio himself says that Dante was most abstemious in respect of food, drink, and sleep, sternly rebuking those who thought much about "what they should eat or what they should drink," by saying that they appeared "not to eat that they might live, but to live that they might eat." Moreover Boccaccio says that Dante's own food was of the plainest description (*il più si pasceva di grossi*). Lionardo says that he was fond of associating with young men whose thoughts turned on love, and that he was himself much occupied with the same passion, "*non per libidine ma per gentilezza di core*". Manetti makes a similar reservation. F. Villani states very explicitly that Dante was "vitae *continentissimae*, cibi potusque parcissimus". Apart from such direct statements as these of Lionardo and Villani, it seems scarcely likely that one who exercised severe and habitual self-restraint in most bodily pleasures should have abandoned himself with little or no restraint to another, to say nothing of the incongruity of such a life as Boccaccio implies with the tone and spirit of his writings, with his general severity of character, or even, let us add, with his features and expression, in the accurate preservation of which he, though dead, seems still to plead and protest against this unworthy accusation.

There is another " quality ", though not indeed a " defect ", of Dante's character which should be briefly noticed ; I mean his strict sense of justice and stern impartiality.   This was shown in a remarkable manner during his tenure of the Priorate, when the sentence of banishment was carried out by him with rigid impartiality upon his own political and personal friends, notably among the latter Guido Cavalcanti, who was very dear to him, and was already in almost a dying state.   The *Divina Commedia* abounds with illustrations of this.   Dante may have been mistaken in his judgments in assigning both the rewards and punishments of the other world, but he is beyond all suspicion of making his verdicts the vehicle for gratifying either personal hate or friendship. I need only mention such prominent examples as that of his own Master, Brunetto Latini, of whom Dante, though placing him in Hell, speaks with such tender and touching affection.   On the other hand he admits to Purgatory one whom he so much detested as Charles of Anjou, and whom personally he would no doubt have willingly " delivered over to Satan ".   Further, there is, I believe, only one single instance of his placing any personal friend in Paradise, viz. Carlo Martello, the son of Charles the Lame, " the cripple of Jerusalem ".

Another subject of great interest in regard to Dante, one on which his biographers throw no

light, though his own writings do, is his attitude
in respect of Religious Belief and Doubt. I can
really do little more than give it a passing allusion now. By many he has been regarded as a
heretic and a freethinker, no doubt owing to the
trenchant and uncompromising denunciations of
the abuses of the Roman Church in his day.
That Church however has never condemned him,
if we except the partial and hesitating condemnation of the local Inquisition at Madrid in 1614,
by which three passages were put upon the Index.
The *De Monarchia* has indeed been proscribed,
but that is on the ground of political rather than
religious heresy, and Boccaccio mentions that the
Cardinal Legate of Romagna, the French Cardinal
Bertrand de Poyet, purposed to burn the bones of
Dante, as a heretic, together with his book *De
Monarchia*, and was with very great difficulty
deterred from his purpose. During his lifetime
(as might naturally be expected) Dante was
denounced as a heretic by persons who did not
agree with him, and the composition known as
the "Credo" of Dante—*Io scrissi già d'amor più
volte rime*—is traditionally said to have been
written as a refutation of the charge. This is
likely enough, though there is not much reason
to suppose that Dante was *himself* the author of
these verses.[1] I have generally put a restraint

[1] Indeed in two or three old MSS. they are definitely
assigned to Antonio da Ferrara, and such is the opinion
of Apostolo Zeno, Allacci and Mortara. (See *Catal. Bodl.
MSS.* p. 113.)

upon myself in respect of the repetition of traditional anecdotes when not found in the early biographers, because, as we have already seen, and
shall again have occasion to point out, they are so
utterly untrustworthy, but I must take leave to
quote that which relates to the composition of
the "Credo," or rather (since there are two or
three versions of it) one that I came across when
examining a MS. at Rome in the Biblioteca
Casanatense,[1] partly because it is very graphic in
its details, more so than the forms of the story
generally given, and partly because I do not
suppose it has ever been printed.[2]   It relates that
Dante was one morning walking along to the
Church of S. Francis (at Ravenna of course) when
he was met by a worthy Friar, a Master in
Theology and also an Inquisitor, who addressed
him thus : "Are you that fantastical Dante (*quel
Dante fantastico*) who pretends to have visited
Hell, Purgatory, and Heaven ? "   And Dante
with great reverence replied : "I am Dante "
(*Io son Dante*).   (The form and manner of this
reply is at least *ben trovato*.)   Then the Friar
said : "Dante, Dante, you would have done better
to have written a book on Grammar and established yourself in the Church of God, and not go

---

[1] Batines, No. 344.

[2] Fraticelli gives a different form of the legend from a MS.
in the Bibl. Riccard. at Florence, No. 142 in Batines.
There are also two forms in Papanti, *Dante secondo la
Tradizione*, etc., pp. 46, etc.

about making poetry and sonnets and rubbish (*non andare facendo rime, nè sonetti, nè frasche*). And Dante, well armed as he was, wished to make his defence, but the Inquisitor said : "You shall reply to me in two days hence, because it is now too late to dispute about the Christian faith." (This is curious, as the incident was said to have occurred in the morning.) Then Dante replied that he would do so willingly. At the time appointed Dante returned with the "Professione di Fede," *Io scrissi*, etc., and the Inquisitor had nothing more to say, but gave Dante his blessing, and Dante after that paid no more heed to him (*et Dante non curò più de' suoi fatti*).

But though Dante was certainly not a "heretic", but a man of very strong and fervent faith (as many passages in the *Paradiso* abundantly prove, and especially that Canto in which he is examined by S. Peter on the subject of his Faith (as he is elsewhere by S. James in reference to Hope, and by S. John in reference to Charity), yet his was by no means a blind faith. He exercised certainly, and claimed distinctly, the right of private judgment. No less than three times in the *Paradiso* does he distinctly place the *rational* grounds of faith and duty before that of *authority* (*Par.* xxiv. 133; xxvi. 25 and 46. See also xix. 103-9, and xx. 127-9). There is also, I think, clear evidence that he had fought his way to Faith through Doubt, and that he passed through

a period of painful mental conflict.[1]   Not to cite
passages that might be quoted from the *Convito*,
my own belief is that the reproaches of Beatrice,
to which we have already referred, relate to *intellectual* not *moral* aberrations, infidelity to the
ideal Beatrice, who represented Theology or
Revealed Truth.   It would take far too long now
to attempt to prove this.   I may perhaps be able
to return to the subject on a future occasion, and
also to another point which is sometimes mentioned in connection with the subject of Dante's
orthodoxy ; I mean, the peculiarity of his treatment of the sin of Heresy.   I should rather say
his non-treatment of it, from which it has been inferred that he had some sympathy, if not for heresy
itself, at least for the right of individual judgment, of which it was the exaggeration.   We may
observe (1) heresy has no place or mention in
Purgatory, though perhaps the Church rather than
Dante would be responsible for this : and (2) in
the Inferno we have the authors of *schism* punished with great severity, and in a place low down
in Hell, but we do not find *heresy* or intellectual
doubt, *as such*, to be the subject of any special
punishment.   A small number of " Heresiarchs "
are punished, it is true, not heretics generally,
but only the peculiar form of unbelief of which
Epicurus *e tutti i suoi seguaci* were the type,
who denied the Immortality of the Soul, in fact,
Materialists,

---

[1] I have collected a good many passages bearing on this
subject in a letter to the *Academy* of Nov. 15th, 1879.

"Che l' anima col corpo morta fanno."

These are placed also in a curious and exceptional position, outside the walls of the City of Dis, and outside, too, of the general classification of sins into those of Incontinence, Violence, and Fraud; being, so to speak, intercalated between the first two of these. Such a typical heretic as Averrhoes (occurring as he does so frequently in mediæval art) is with the virtuous heathen in Limbo. So also is Avicenna. Such prominent offenders in this direction as Abelard and Arnold of Brescia are not mentioned at all. But I can only hint at these anomalies, and the inference as to Dante's mental attitude that has sometimes been drawn from them, since I cannot pursue the subject further now.

We are not left entirely to conjecture and inference, or to external information, as to Dante's character or failings, since even in the *Divina Commedia* itself there are certain passages in which he confesses to some definite faults, though, as I have already said, all such admissions are to be received with a certain amount of caution. Besides the celebrated scene in *Purg.* xxx., where he is overwhelmed with the pitiless storm of the reproaches of Beatrice (whatever may be their true meaning), he makes the following more or less definite confessions. The most precise of these (as we might perhaps expect) is to the sin of pride. This indeed recurs several times. (1) In *Purg.* xi., after the splendid de-

L

scription of the vanity of all human fame, put
into the mouth of Oderisi d'Agobbio (already
referred to), he declares in line 118 that these
words have inspired him with true humility,
and have assuaged a great swelling of pride
within him.   Moreover, in the same Canto (l. 78)
he represents himself as already sharing in the
punishment of that *Cornice*: *A me, che tutto
chin con lui* (al. *loro*) *andava.*   Comp. xii. 8, 9,
In xii. 118 he speaks of the enormous sense of
relief which he suddenly felt without under-
standing why, and it is explained to be due to
the removal of the first of the seven P's that had
been stamped upon his forehead by the angel, viz.
that corresponding to the sin of pride.   Did this
passage stand alone, however, it might be explained as having a general reference to pride
being the root and source of all other sins in
man, as is often expressed by theologians.[1]   But
we find a very definite personal accusation on
this subject occurring in the next Canto, viz. xiii.
133-8, where on the next *Cornice* (that of Envy)
he confesses that he must expiate that sin himself when his time comes, though it will not be for
long, since his offences in that respect have not
been serious, but his mind is greatly distressed
at the thought of the torment that he will have
to undergo in the lower division of Purgatory

---

[1] See, *inter alia*, Ecclus. x. 13, and S. Thomas Aquinas
(ii. 2, Q. 162, Art. 6). Also Boethius, Augustine, and Isidore
quoted (*l.c.*) by S. Thomas.

(that where pride is punished), so that even already he feels the weight of it oppressing him.[1] Having thus confessed to much pride and to some tinge of envy, he passed unscathed apparently through the next three *Cornici*, his conscience not accusing him of Anger,[2] " Accidia," or Avarice. In the *Cornice* of Gluttony (No. vi.) there is considerable doubt as to the interpretation of a passage (*Purg.* xxiii. 116) in which Dante clearly accuses himself of having led, with Forese Donati his kinsman, a life on which he looked back with shame. This has been taken by some as a general reference, either to a worldly life, or possibly a politically misguided life, since he says in the following lines that Virgil had delivered him from such a life the day before yesterday (in reference to the *selva oscura* of *Inf.* i.); while by others it has been supposed to have special reference to the sin of Gluttony, which is that for which Forese and others in this *Cornice* are being especially punished. Moreover, in the next Canto, the question of Forese,

---

[1] See Benvenuto, quoted in Supplementary Notes.

[2] Unless we suppose (as has sometimes been maintained) that *Purg.* xv. 130-2 involves an admission of some guiltiness in respect of anger. The story in Boccaccio's *Vita*, c. 12, might be mentioned, of Dante's fury (*insania*) when any one attacked the Ghibellines in his presence, so that even if it were a woman or a little boy he would throw stones at them. This, whether true or not, is introduced as *publichissima cosa in Romagna.* Filelfo (if indeed he is worth quoting) describes him as *excandescens aliquando, sed nequaquam iracundus, sed non nisi gravissimis incendebatur causis.*

how soon should he see Dante there again, has
been taken to confirm this view, and to amount
to an indirect confession that he would have to
expiate the sin of gluttony himself hereafter.
Whether or no, the answer of Dante makes no
such definite admission. He merely replies, " I
know not how long I have to live, but, however
speedy my return, it will not outstrip my desire
to come" (ll. 76-8).

It is perhaps curious to note that both Boccaccio and Villani mention that though Dante
was himself most abstemious in respect of food,
and most plain in his own diet, he admired good
cooking. " *Li delicati (cibi) lodava*," says Boccaccio (which is repeated in Latin by Manetti).
Villani says that he was " *lautae delicataeque lauda-
tor vitae*," while himself most inconsistently living
on coarse fare.

On the last *Cornice* of Purgatory, where Lust
is punished, we are naturally much interested
to see whether Dante makes any confessions
which throw any light upon the serious charge
brought against him by his biographers, and Boccaccio in particular. As to this two points occur
to us. (1) His candid admissions in other cases
very much enhance the force of any argument
that might be drawn from the absence of such
admissions here, if so it should be. (2) If the
strong language of Boccaccio even *approximately*
represents the truth, we should expect admissions
and confessions of a peculiarly strong and un-

equivocal character. But now what is the case? We may read carefully through Cantos xxvi. and xxvii. and yet we shall not find a word of self-reproach, not even when he meets with Guido Guinicelli, with whom he has so warm a greeting (xxvi. 92, etc.). It is common to quote the fact that Dante has to pass through the purifying fire as an admission that he needed special purgation from this particular sin. But it is to be observed that this is represented as a *general,* and, as we might say, *physical,* necessity, rather than a *personal* one. The Angel in xxvii. 10 says that *no one* can pass forward except through the fire. Note particularly that the same necessity applies to Virgil and Statius quite as much as to Dante (see xxvii. 46-7). The approach to the Terrestrial Paradise lies through this wall of fire (no doubt in recollection of Gen. iii. 24). We ought perhaps to mention here, in passing, the inference that has been commonly drawn from *Inf.* xvi. 106-8, where the *corda* is generally interpreted to mean the adoption of the vows of the Franciscan order, as a help to conquer the temptations of "*lussuria,*" symbolised by the "*lonza alla pelle dipinta.*" Again, *Inf.* i. 34-6 has been thought to point in the same direction, when Dante refers to the serious obstruction caused to his onward progress by the "*lonza.*" But it would seem that the other two "*fiere*" hindered him still more, and as this was certainly not the case with avarice, or rather cupidity (*lupa*), per-

haps the personal application of the passage must
not be too closely pressed. The confessions, whatever they may mean, made through the reproaches
of Beatrice in Canto xxx. occur *after* Purgatory
is passed, and all the seven P's removed by ex-
piation. If therefore they referred to sins of
literal unfaithfulness, in Boccaccio's sense, they
would be somewhat inartistically dealt with entirely out of their proper place, and *after* they
had been already purged. For this, as well as
many other reasons, it is much more likely that
they refer to spiritual unfaithfulness, to aberrations from the revealed truth into the paths of
philosophy and human knowledge.

Dante certainly does appear at one period of
his life to have betaken himself to these " broken
cisterns " in place of the wellspring of Revelation
or Theology typified by Beatrice. If this is that
of which he has accused himself, through the
mouth of Beatrice, the place chosen would at
least be appropriate, since it was just that sort of
Pride of Intellect and the ill-regulated desire of
the knowledge of good and evil that caused the
loss of that Earthly Paradise (then by him re-
gained) in the first instance. So at least Dante
himself held. See *Par.* xxvi. 115-17 :—

> " non il gustar del legno
> Fu per sè la cagion di tanto esilio,
> Ma solamente il trapassar del segno."

So again, in a passage already quoted, the cause of

Eve's offence is represented as being her unwillingness to remain "*sotto alcun velo*" (*Purg.* xxix. 27; see also *Par.* vii. 97-100). But, as I have said before, I must not be tempted to enter into this discussion further now.

The anecdotal literature about Dante, mostly anonymous and scattered among unedited MSS. and minor Novellieri, has been fully treated by Papanti, *Dante secondo la Tradizione e i Novellatori* (Livorno, 1873). Many of these stories are sufficiently amusing, but the large majority are undoubtedly apocryphal, since they are told elsewhere, and often long previously, in connection with other well-known names. We have seen already how one of the best known comes from Macrobius, another is found in Athenaeus, another (as we shall see presently) in Josephus; others occur in ancient folk-lore common even to other countries besides Italy. No doubt a great and commanding figure like that of Dante has a tendency, like a magnet, to attract to itself the anonymous anecdotes that are floating about, as it were unattached, in the popular conversation and literature. One of these stories is such a venerable literary "Joe Miller" as to be found almost *totidem verbis* in Josephus![1] The courtiers of Ptolemy Euergetes played upon Hyrcanus at a feast the same practical joke that is repeated

---

[1] See Josephus, *Ant. Jud.* xii. c. iv. § 9. The story as told of Dante is given by Papanti, *Dante secondo la Tradizione*, etc., p. 91.

about Dante at the court of Can Grande, viz. they managed to get the collected bones from the plates of the guests all deposited beside him. In each case attention was then drawn to the fact in the way of derision. The repartee in each case is the same, viz. that "whereas dogs devour both meat and bones, as the other guests have apparently done, men eat the meat only, and leave the bones, and this is what I, being a man, have now done." Another version of Dante's reply is that if he had been a big dog (*can grande*) he might have eaten them. It was probably the name of Can Grande that first suggested the transference of this venerable joke to Dante, either in this adapted version or in its old and unaltered form. I mention this as an illustration how such stories are manufactured. But I am sure, as I said at the outset, that we may go too far in the direction of scepticism. We are rather apt to pride ourselves nowadays on the ruthless scepticism by which we strip off all the flowers and embellishments, or (as a recent brilliant writer has called them) the "mock-pearls" of history, and leave, as we flatter ourselves, nothing but solid and well-established facts. It may be doubted whether we do not sometimes go further, and leave ourselves with the skeleton rather than the body, having stripped off not only the adornments, but even the skin and flesh of history. Or, to change the metaphor, in our eagerness to get rid of the tares we "root up sometimes the wheat with them." As Macaulay has very well said : " A more exact narrative is perhaps given by the writer; it may be doubted whether more exact notions are conveyed to the reader." In these old gossiping records and traditions " something may be lost in accuracy, but much is gained in effect ". Let this be our apology for having lingered a little over the biographical and anecdotal side of the great poet's record, comforting ourselves with a sentiment, often forgotten in theology as well as in history, that that which is, in the strict logical sense, " *not proved* " is not therefore " *disproved* ".

SUPPLEMENTARY NOTES.

The following seem to be the best-known or most accessible Editions of the *Vita* and the *Compendio* [from the *Bibliografia* of Macrì-Leone's Introduction, where he enumerates twenty Editions of the *Vita* and four of the *Compendio*]:—

VITA.

(1) Ed. Bartolommeo Gamba : Venezia, 1825.

(2) Vol. xv. of the *Opere volgari di Boccaccio*, ed. Moutier : Firenze, 1833.

(3) Ed. Lauriel : Napoli, 1856.

(4) Prefixed to the *Comento* of Boccaccio ; ed. Milanesi, Le Monnier : Firenze, 1863.

(5) Ed. Ant. Gual. de Marzo : Firenze, 1864.

(6) We should of course add Macrì-Leone's own Edition : Firenze, 1888.

COMPENDIO.

(1) In Vol. v. of the *Divina Commedia* : Padova, Tip. della Minerva, 1822.

(2) In the *Opere volgari di Dante*; ed. Ciardetti : Firenze, 1830-32.

(3) Prefixed to the *Divina Commedia* published by Didot : Paris, 1844.

P. 4. Benvenuto da Imola, the pupil and devoted admirer of Boccaccio, composed his very valuable Commentary as Lecturer at Bologna. See the interesting reference to this in his comment on *Purg.* xv. 60. His work abounds with kindly, and even affectionate, references to Boccaccio, whose lectures at Florence he himself attended. See the description of the condition of the

Church of San Stefano (on *Par.* xv. 97), "quae hodie est satis inordinata et neglecta, *ut vidi dum audirem venerabilem meum praeceptorem Boccaccium de Certaldo legentem istum nobilem poetam in dicta ecclesia*".

P. 9. It may be worth while comparing the statements of the early biographers with the limited information given to us (and them) by Dante himself in *Par.* xv. and xvi.

He does not go back further than Cacciaguida, his great-great-grandfather, either in respect of the names, or the place of origin of his ancestors. See *Par.* xvi. 40-5. The language of the latter *terzina* is remarkable, and its meaning is still a matter of dispute :—

> ' Basti de' miei maggiori udirne questo;;
> Chi ei si furo, ed onde venner quivi,
> Più è tacer, che ragionare, onesto."

As to Cacciaguida himself, Dante makes him say that he had a *brother* called "Eliseo," and that his own wife came to him from the valley of the Po. This is a sufficiently vague topographical indication to be consistent with the conflicting claims of Ferrara (Boccaccio), Parma (Villani), and Verona (Dionisi). It has naturally been inferred that Dante's own knowledge did not extend further back than Cacciaguida. It has sometimes been argued that in *Inf.* xv. 70-8 he means to imply a Roman origin for his family (so Boccaccio, Villani, etc.), but the inference is very inconclusive, as his words seem to refer to the inhabitants of Florence generally, *la bellissima e famosissima figlia di Roma (Conv.* i. 3). Lionardo says that Dante appears to indicate *in alcuni luoghi* that his ancestors were among the original Roman founders of Florence. But he does not give a hint where these *alcuni luoghi* are to be found, and his usual caution reappears when he adds: *Ma questa è cosa molto incerta, e secondo mio parere, niente è altro che indovinare.*

Manetti, as we might expect, is troubled by no such scruples, and boldly begins his Life with the assertion

Dantes Poeta clarissimus ex urbe Roma, ut ipse QUODAM LOCO *innuere videtur, originem traxit.* The old chronicler Ricordano Malespini improves upon them all by saying not only that Dante was descended from the Frangipani, but that that family itself was descended from an older Eliseo or Elisone, who was the brother-in-law, and one of the seven companions, of one Uberto Cesare, who founded Florence at the command of Julius Caesar!

Dante makes Cacciaguida say that his son, and consequently Dante's great-grandfather, is still detained on the 1st *Cornice* of Purgatory, expiating the sin of Pride (*Par.* xv. 91-6). Of him nothing whatever appears to be known, and this reference to him is curious, since Dante himself makes no mention of him among those whom he met with on that *Cornice.*

The subject of Dante's ancestry will be found further discussed in Scartazzini's *Abhandlungen*, No. i., "Dante's Abstammung und Adel"; Fraticelli's *Vita di Dante*, Ch. i.; Pelli's *Memorie*, Sect. iii.

Pp. 9, 40, 83, etc. The confusion between Attila and Totila was common in Dante's time, and among such chroniclers as he had access to. As a matter of fact, Florence was destroyed by Totila, king of the Goths, c. 540 A.D., and not by Attila, king of the Huns, who was called *flagellum Dei* (see *Inf.* xii. 134), and who died 453. Dante attributes the destruction of Florence to Attila (*Inf.* xiii. 149), Ricordano Malespini, *Hist. Fior.* cxxi., ascribes it to *Atile sive Totile flagellum Dei.* Villani attributes the destruction to *Totile flagellum Dei* (ii. c. 1).[1] Boccaccio, as we have seen, in the *Vita* refers to Attila, "the most cruel king of the Vandals," while in the *Comento* (ii. p. 305) he speaks of him, on the authority of Paulus Diaconus, as king of the Goths, and though recognising that

---

[1] In one of the Brit. Mus. MSS. Totila is substituted for Attila in *Inf.* xii. 134, possibly from a recollection of these words of Villani. The language of the *Ottimo Comento* on xiii. 149 seems to recognise this reading as occurring in the preceding Canto.

Totila is also mentioned as the destroyer of Florence, wrongly maintains that it was not Totila, but Attila. In p. 355 he professes to quote Villani as his authority for the same statement, though Villani rightly says Totila, while wrongly describing him as *flagellum Dei.*

Among the older commentaries, the *Ottimo* speaks of Attila as king of the Vandals, and in reference to *Inf.* xiii. 149 notices the differences of opinion as to whether Attila or Totila was the name of the destroyer of Florence, adding that some suppose that they were both names of the same man! The *Anonimo Fiorentino* in his note on xiii. 149 speaks without further explanation of *Totile flagellum Dei,* and in that on xii. 134 he states that in 440 there was a king of the *Vandals and Goths* called *Totila.* He then proceeds at great length to give his history, which is a general mixture of events connected with Attila and Totila, chiefly the former, whose name is twice substituted for that of Totila in the course of the narrative. Benvenuto da Imola on xiii. 149 introduces the story of the destruction of Florence by *Attila flagellum Dei,* with a cautious reservation, *si tamen verum est,* and he concludes by saying that Attila in fact appears never to have crossed the Apennines, nor does Paulus Diaconus or any other author say that he did so. He concludes :—*Ideo dico quod auctor noster secutus est chronicas patriae sua, quae multa frivola similia dicunt.* It is important to remember this in many other places, where Dante has been charged with historical inaccuracies, in other words, with not having availed himself of the researches of later generations.

P. 11. The selection by Dante of "Orazio satiro" as one of the five great poets of antiquity is familiar to every one (*Inf.* iv. 89). I cannot however find much evidence of Dante's familiarity with his works, at any rate beyond the limits of the *Ars Poetica,* or *La Poetria,* as Dante calls it. That is quoted four times by Dante, as follows :—(1) l. 70, in *Conv.* ii. 14, earlier lines (60-2) of the same passage being also evidently copied in *Par.* xxvi. 137 ; (2) l. 141 in *Vita*

Nuova, c. 25, where Virgil, Ovid, and Lucan are also
referred to, and Dante notes that the quotation of Horace
carries with it practically the authority of Homer[1] also, so
that his five great poets are again united here ; (3) l. 38 in
De Vulg. Eloq. ii. 4 ; (4) ll. 93-5 in the Epistle to Can
Grande, § 10.   It has been argued that the list of Roman
poets in *Purg.* xxii. 97-8 is probably suggested by Horace,
either *Epist.* ii. i. 58-9, or *Ars Poet.* l. 54, and I have
discussed this in my work on *Textual Criticism,* p. 412.
There is also a vague reference to Horace by name, but not
a direct quotation, in *Conv.* iv. 12.   As far as I am aware,
there are no other passages in which Horace is quoted or
imitated.   The case is very different in regard to Virgil,
Ovid, and Statius.

Pp. 11 and 54.   Though I have twice noticed that
Boccaccio is the sole authority for the identification of the
Beatrice of Dante with Beatrice Portinari, I must not be
supposed thereby to indicate the least doubt as to the trustworthiness of that statement, or of the literal and historical
reality of Beatrice.   This question has been much contro-
verted, and particularly of late years, with an increasing
tendency (I think) to regard her as a pure myth.   I have
no intention of entering into this controversy here, but I
must point out that Boccaccio made his very definite statements, both as to her parentage and marriage, within fifty
years of Dante's death, in his Lectures before a Florentine
audience, which probably contained, as Florence itself certainly did, many members, connections, or friends of both
of the families of which he spoke, the Portinari and the
Bardi.   Both were still extant, and well known in Florence,
"their houses are with us unto this day", and the Bardi
were a family of even European reputation as bankers.
Besides, if Boccaccio were inventing, why should he contrive
the gratuitous improbability of making Beatrice a married
woman at all, to say nothing of marrying her into one of

[1] Referred to as *il buono Omero,* which itself perhaps recalls
Hor. *Ars Poet.* l. 359.

the best-known families of Florence. It is to my mind in-conceivable that Boccaccio should have publicly committed himself to a statement, the falsity of which, if false, must have been so glaring and palpable that its assertion could only have covered him with ridicule. I purposely omit other considerations, which appear to me almost equally strong, because they do not arise out of the subject-matter of the present book. I will only add that I do not abandon my belief, even when I see Beatrice described (as by a recent German writer on the subject)[1] as *die Frau Bardi, geb. Portinari* !

The meaning and construction of the passage from the *Vita Nuova* quoted in the text, p. 11, seems to be illustrated by a very similar passage in Boccaccio, *Decam.* iii. *Nov.* 10, *il nome per lo quale voi mi chiamate, da tale che* SEPPE BEN CHE SI DIRE *mi fu imposto.*

P. 38. In the *Rime* of Boccaccio there are two curious Sonnets (Nos. vii. and viii.) in which he makes an apology for himself against an anonymous detractor (like Terence replying to the *malevoli veteris poetae maledictis*), first for the coarseness of some of his writings, which he does not indeed defend, but says that he has been sufficiently punished for it by his grievous bodily infirmities (*crudelmente Apollo nel mio corpo l'ha vengiate*, etc.) ; secondly, for his *Comento*, wherein he has expounded Dante's sublime work to the unworthy herd : as to which he consoles him-self that it will not be of much use to them ! The latter sonnet is sufficiently curious, in reference to the work referred to in the text, to be worth reproducing here—

> " Se Dante piange, dove ch'el si sia,
> Che li concetti del suo alto ingegno
> Aperti sieno stati al vulgo indegno,
> Come tu di' della Lettura mia,

---

[1] It is perhaps worth mentioning that Boccaccio's own father, on one at any rate of his visits to Paris, was travelling as an agent of the Bardi. (See Crescini, *Studi sul Boccaccio.* p. 10.)

> Ciò mi dispiace molto, nè mai fia
>   Ch' io non ne porti verso me disdegno,
>   Come che alquanto pur me ne ritengo,
>   Perchè d'altrui, non mia, fu tal follia.
> Vana speranza, e vera povertate,
>   E l' abbagliato senno degli amici,
>   E gli loro preghi ciò mi fecer fare :
> Ma non godevan guar di tal derrate
>   Questi ingrati meccanici, nimici
>   D' ogni leggiadro e caro adoperare !"

This would seem to imply that, from whatever cause (perhaps sudden and severe illness) the *Comento* was suspended, some interval elapsed before the author's death.

P. 49. The family of Boccaccio came from Certaldo, but they had become Florentines two generations earlier. It will be remembered that Dante (in the mouth of Cacciaguida) deplores the extension of Florentine citizenship, and singles out Certaldo as one of the villages from which the *gente nuova* was derived :—

> "Ma la cittadinanza, ch' è or mista
>   Di Campi, e *di Certaldo*, e di Fighine,
>   Pura vedeasi nell' ultimo artista.
> O quanto fora meglio esser vicine
>   Quelle genti ch' io dico," etc.[1]

(Compare *Inferno*, xvi. 73.) The actual place of Boccaccio's birth has been much disputed, but most authorities now agree that it was neither Certaldo nor Florence, but Paris, his mother being a Frenchwoman, with whom his father had formed an intrigue while on a visit there on business in 1312-13. Boccaccio might at any rate then plead the excuse of the young Greek scapegrace for his irregularities of life, " συγγενὲς γὰρ ἡμῖν " (Ar. *Nic. Eth.* VII. vi.). The question of Boccaccio's birthplace has been exhaustively discussed recently by Crescini, *Studi sul Boccaccio*, 1887.

P. 55. It might be objected that since, in his *Comento* (*Lez.* I. p. 322, etc.), Boccaccio surprises us with almost as

---

[1] *Par.* xvi. 49, etc.

minute a biography of Homer, his appearance, his character, his habits, and small incidents of his life, as though he were a contemporary Florentine, this may be taken as a measure of his trustworthiness in respect of Dante. This, however, would not be fair. It would prove Boccaccio to be devoid of much critical faculty, but not necessarily to be a romancer. He no doubt followed (as any one then would have done) some or any of those fabulous romances which were commonly accepted as sober history in the middle ages, *quod unum apud illos memoriae et annalium genus erat* (Tac.). There is no reason to suppose that he invented on his own account. Again, an author is consciously in a very different position when writing about one of such recent date that he might very nearly have known him personally, while many were still living who did so, and when he is trying what can be said about those

"Quorum Flaminia tegitur cinis atque Latina".

P. 60. It has been suggested that the *modernus quidam* of Villani is none other than Benvenuto da Imola. For in his *Introductio*, p. 12, the latter says that Dante's family name was derived from Ferrara, in proof of which he quotes *Par.* xv. 137, adding (with very imperfect logic), *Constat autem Ferrariam esse in valle Padi.* It is obvious to remark with Villani—*quasi sola Ferraria in valle Padi sita sit, et non Parma.* Moreover, the Introduction and the whole Commentary is addressed in the way of dedication *ad clarissimum Principem Nicolaum Marchionem Estensem*, etc. It should be mentioned, however, that Villani when speaking of this *modernus* uses the expression " POETICO *adfirmans commento*," and qualifies the reference to *Par.* xv. 137 by saying " *ex eo fortasse loco argumentum mutuatus* ".

P. 101. It seems more probable that Filelfo, *tardo e mendace biografo*, as Bartoli calls him, has erred in excess rather than in defect (as implied in the text) respecting the family attributed to Dante. The six sons referred to

M

above, p. 101, seem to appear first in the pages of Pelli (*Memorie*), and some of them on very slender evidence indeed. This (like much else), when once asserted, is generally repeated by later writers, as if it were well established and undisputed history. In fact, Aliger and Eliseus (two highly suspicious names) appear to rest solely on this passage in Filelfo, and it is significant that he has taken the precaution to clear thᴗm off at an early age, so that no inconvenient precision of details respecting their lives need be required. Gabriello and Bernardo have a still more shadowy hold on existence. For the former, a seventeenth-century writer is made to vouch ; as far as the latter, οὐδεὶς οἶδεν ἐξ ὅτου 'φάνη (see Bartoli, *Lett. Ital.* v. pp. 106-7). It is probable that these may have been nephews, sons of Dante's brother Francesco, who have strayed across into the better-known family. Bartoli adds that there exists one document, giving evidence of a daughter, Antonia, otherwise unknown, as well as Beatrice (p. 108). So that the poet's family seems to reduce itself to four,—Pietro, Jacopo, Beatrice, and Antonia. Manetti speaks merely of *plures liberi*, but prudently leaves the numbers vague and the names blank. This rectification of the list of Dante's children is interesting, as bearing on the alleged charge of his neglect of his family, as well as of his wife, from the moment of his exile, since there is distinct evidence of the presence of Pietro, Jacopo, and Beatrice at Ravenna.

P. 109. It should be added that Villani was at any rate old enough to visit Rome on the occasion of the Jubilee in 1300, since he states that what he saw there first inspired him with the idea of writing the history of his own city Florence, *figluola e fattura di Roma* (*Cron.* viii. 36), and further, that he actually commenced it in that year (*Così negli anni* 1300 *tornato da Roma, cominciai a compilare questo libro*). There are moreover very strong reasons for supposing Dante also to have been at Rome then (see my *Time-References*, p. 114).

P. 113. The whole passage is worth quoting, since it will be seen that it places this alleged visit in Dante's *youth*. This is inconsistent with Boccaccio's own distinct statements, not only in the *Vita*, but also in the *Comento* (see i. p. 88, ed. 1863), where he attributes the journey to the hopelessness of his return to Florence, *avendo alquanti anni circuita Italia*. This makes the genuineness of the poetical Epistle itself very doubtful, slight as its value as evidence on this point would be in any case. The passage runs thus :—

> "Traxerit ut *juvenem* Phoebus per celsa nivosi
> Cyrrheos, mediosque sinus, tacitosque recessus
> Naturae, caelique vias, terraeque, marisque,
> Aonios fontes, Parnassi culmen, et antra
> Julia, Parisios dudum, extremosque Britannos."

It is more probable that Boccaccio (if really the author) thus poetically expresses the wide extent of Dante's wanderings by inserting what he probably regarded as the *ultima Thule* of civilisation. Compare in illustration a curious passage in his *Comento* (*Lez.* vi. vol. i. p. 192), where Boccaccio says that as the course of Empire, Science, and Religion has passed westwards from Assyria to the Medes and Persians, thence in succession to Egypt, Greece, and Rome, and thence still later to the Germans and Franks, "par già che il cielo ne minacci di portarle in Inghilterra"!

P. 123. The case suggested in the text is not after all wholly imaginary. The clever and eccentric Hardouin, that "orbis literati portentum", wrote a pamphlet entitled *Doutes proposés sur l'âge du Dante*, to prove from internal evidence that the *Divina Commedia* could not have been written by Dante, but was the forgery of some disciple of Wyclif about the beginning of the fifteenth century! This curious work is excessively rare. It was privately reprinted in a very small number by C[harles] L[yell] in 1847, from a MS. copy made for him by a friend.

It may be worth while, therefore, to give here some specimen of the arguments of this "curiosity of literature". A
note of admiration is generally more than a sufficient reply
to them.

1. S. Thomas Aquinas appears among the Saints, though
not canonised till 1323. But Dante of course here boldly
anticipates the judgment of the Church, just as (probably)
in the case of Celestine he has reversed it.

2. *Par.* xxvii. 61-3 is said to describe the entrance of
Lewis of Bavaria into Rome in 1328 to set up the Antipope
Nicolas v. in opposition to John XXII. It is scarcely
necessary to remark that this is a pure assumption.

3. He actually employs as an argument the mistake
about Attila in *Inf.* xiii. 149, since (as he falsely asserts)
"all the historians attest positively that Attila never set
foot in Tuscany"! (See *sup.* p. 172.)

4. He states quite falsely, and as far as I can see irrele-
vantly for the purposes of argument, that Plautus and
Terence and Agathon (*entre autres un nommé Agathon
que personne ne connoît!*) are in Purgatory. See the
contrary stated in *Purg.* xxii. 100-8.

5. The poem abounds with wrong and heretical views on
various subjects, and particularly with Wyclifist denunciations (*emportements Wiclifistes*) against the Papacy.

Apart from the ludicrous weakness or falsity of these
so-called arguments, did it never occur to a clever and
learned man, as Hardouin certainly was, that (1) many
MSS. of the *Divina Commedia* much earlier than 1400
actually exist; and (2) that several Commentaries were
written in the course of the fourteenth century upon the
supposed non-existent poem?

P. 129, Note 2. Benvenuto da Imola's Comment on this
passage is sufficiently quaint to deserve quotation : "Sicut
enim gravitas et modestia decet sapientem in actibus et
verbis, sic et incessu. Velocitas enim est magis negotia-
torum et mercatorum, quam philosophorum et poetarum :

et vere videre Virgilium currere per illam planitiem et Dantem post eum cum sua ampla toga deberet praestare materiem risus etiam illi rigido Catoni "!

P. 130. Dante would evidently have agreed with the sentiment of the author of the Book of Ecclesiasticus : " A man's attire and excessive laughter and gait shew what he is " (xix. 30).

P. 163. Benvenuto's Comment here again is curious : " And here observe that our poet was from his youth proud by reason of his birth, learning, and good position, but assuredly he bore his burden in this life, the burden, I mean, of exile, poverty, and the envy of others. And certainly, I venture to say in good conscience the very same of myself, namely, that I have been sometimes more proud than envious ; 'sed certe jam bene portavi saxum in mundo '."

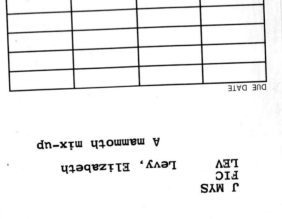

DUE DATE

J MYS
FIC
LEV   Levy, Elizabeth
A mammoth mix-up